Innocence
and Estrangement
in the Fiction of
Jean Stafford

Innocence and Estrangement in the Fiction of Jean Stafford

MAUREEN RYAN

LOUISIANA STATE UNIVERSITY PRESS
BATON ROUGE AND LONDON

Designer: Sylvia Malik Loftin
Typeface: Century Expanded
Typesetter: G & S Typesetters, Inc.
Printer: Thomson-Shore, Inc.
Binder: John Dekker & Sons, Inc.

10 9 8 7 6 5 4 3 2 1

Excerpts from *Boston Adventure* by Jean Stafford, copyright 1944 by Harcourt Brace Jovanovich, Inc.; renewed 1972 by Jean Stafford. Reprinted by permission of the publisher and Faber and Faber, Ltd. Excerpts from *The Mountain Lion*, copyright © 1947, renewed 1975 by Jean Stafford, printed by permission of Russell & Volkening, Inc., as agents for the author, and by the permission of Chatto & Windus. Excerpts from *The Catherine Wheel* by Jean Stafford. Copyright 1951, 1952 by Jean Stafford. Reprinted by permission of Farrar, Straus and Giroux, Inc. Excerpts from *Bad Characters* by Jean Stafford. Copyright © 1946, 1953, 1954, 1956, 1957, 1964 by Jean Stafford. Reprinted by permission of Farrar, Straus and Giroux, Inc., and of Russell & Volkening, as agents for the author. Excerpts from *The Collected Stories of Jean Stafford*. Copyright © 1944, 1945, 1946, 1948, 1949, 1950, 1951, 1952, 1953, 1954, 1955, 1956, 1958, 1964, 1968, 1969 by Jean Stafford. Reprinted by permission of Farrar, Straus and Giroux, Inc., and by permission of the author and Chatto & Windus.

Quotations from the following stories are printed by permission of Russell & Volkening, Inc., as agents for the author: "And Lots of Solid Color" Copyright © 1939, renewed 1967 by Jean Stafford; "The Cavalier" Copyright © 1949, renewed 1977 by Jean Stafford; "The Connoisseurs" © 1952, renewed 1980 by the estate of Jean Stafford; "The Home Front" Copyright © 1945, renewed 1973 by Jean Stafford; "Miss McKeehan's Pocketbook" Copyright © 1976 by Jean Stafford; "A Slight Maneuver" Copyright © 1946 by Street & Smith Publications Inc. Copyright renewed 1947 by The Conde Nast Publications Inc.; "The Scarlet Letter" Copyright © 1959 by Street & Smith Publications Inc., renewed 1987 by The Conde Nast Publications Inc.; "Souvenirs of Survival" Copyright © 1960 by Street & Smith Publications Inc.; "The Warlock" Copyright © 1955, renewed 1983 by the estate of Jean Stafford; "An Influx of Poets" Copyright © 1978 by Jean Stafford; "A Winter's Tale" Copyright © 1954 by Jean Stafford, renewed 1982 by the estate of Jean Stafford. "The Warlock," "An Influx of Poets," and "The Cavalier" first appeared in the *New Yorker*. Quotations from "The Connoisseurs" also appear courtesy of *Harper's Bazaar*. Quotations from "Truth in Fiction" are reprinted from *Library Journal*, October 1, 1966. Published by R. R. Bowker Co., Div. of Reed Publishing, USA. Copyright © 1966 by Reed Publishing, USA, Div. of Reed Holdings, Inc.

Passages from "Women as Chattels, Men as Chumps" and "Don't Use Ms. with Miss Stafford, Unless You Mean ms.," copyright © 1970/73 by The New York Times Company. Reprinted by permission. Passages from "Woden's Day," by Jean Stafford; "People to Stay," by Nancy Flagg; and "The Interior Castle: The Art of Jean Stafford's Fiction," by Joyce Carol Oates Copyright 1979 by Washington and Lee University, reprinted from *Shenandoah: The Washington and Lee University Review*, with the permission of the Editor. The author also acknowledges *McCall's Magazine* for permission to quote from "Intimations of Hope," and *Saturday Review* for permission to quote from "Wordman, Spare That Tree." Passages from "The Psychological Novel" copyright 1948 by Kenyon College. Reprinted with permission of the author's estate and *Kenyon Review*.

Library of Congress Cataloging-in-Publication Data

Ryan, Maureen, 1953–
  Innocence and estrangement in the fiction of Jean Stafford.

  Bibliography: p.
  Includes index.
    1. Stafford, Jean, 1915–   —Criticism and interpretation.   2. Stafford, Jean, 1915–   —Characters—Women.   3. Women in literature.   I. Title.
PS3569.T2Z85   1987   813'.54   87-2780
ISBN 0-8071-1381-6

For my parents,
Mary Alice White Ryan
and
Leo Edward Ryan

"You're sure you've got your ticket?" says Daisy. "You'll surely be able to get a roomette once you're on."

"I don't know about that," I say. "If there are any V.I.P.s on board, I won't have a chance. 'Spinsters and Orphans Last' is the motto of this line."

—"In the Zoo"

Contents

Preface and Acknowledgments

Herein I explore Jean Stafford's fictional world, examining her thematic interests and technical characteristics. Beginning with the novels and concluding with the short stories, I allude to Stafford's modernist and American sensibilities, and concentrate on her presentation of the experience of women in modern American society. While my reading of Stafford's fiction draws on the work of a number of critics, particularly feminist writers, I have found Annis Pratt's theories in *Archetypal Patterns in Women's Fiction* most useful. Pratt's reliance on myth and her particular interest in the archetypal model of the novel of development, combined with her focus on the genre of fiction, make her work especially applicable to Stafford's vision.

My interest in works written by and about women proceeds from a more fundamental appreciation of literature and my academic training in literary study. For my introduction to the formal study of literature, I thank Theodora R. Graham and Robert J. Graham; for their participation in my graduate study and their guidance and assistance in the early stages of this book, I am grateful to Philip Stevick and Alan Wilde. For their gentle harassment, which helped me along in the revision stage, I thank my colleagues Noel Polk, Peggy Prenshaw, and Elizabeth Inness-Brown; for their support and valuable assistance with the preparation of this book, I owe thanks to Frederick

Barthelme and David H. Roberts, and to Beverly Jarrett, Catherine Barton, and Catherine Landry of Louisiana State University Press. And, for introducing me to Jean Stafford and a wealth of other writers, and teaching me much of what I know about American literature and about how to be a teacher and a scholar, I am indebted to Richard S. Kennedy, my teacher, my colleague, and my friend.

Abbreviations

BA   *Boston Adventure*. New York, 1944.

BC   *Bad Characters*. New York, 1964.

CABS   *Children Are Bored on Sunday*. New York, 1953.

CS   *The Collected Stories of Jean Stafford*. New York, 1969.

CW   *The Catherine Wheel*. New York, 1952.

ML   *The Mountain Lion*. New York, 1947; rpr. Albuquerque, 1972.

*Innocence
and Estrangement
in the Fiction of
Jean Stafford*

Introduction

"Beginnings give me hope. For me, Sundays, not Mondays, are blue."[1] So wrote Jean Stafford in 1971, at the end of a career distinguished by an intense fascination with the Sundays in human lives. Remarkably, the action of a full half of Stafford's stories occurs on Sunday (or Saturday or holidays, days that share the characteristics of Sunday), which allows her to eschew the vicissitudes of the working world and linger over the stages and situations of life that are not defined by money and labor.

Sunday is the end of the weekend, the end of the week, the end; and Stafford explores the end of life with perspicacity tempered by compassion. Her fiction abounds with bitter, eccentric, and charming characters who are responding to the disappointments and solaces of old age. Sunday is too a day of leisure, and Stafford examines throughout her work the aristocratic and the wealthy, those whose lives are not circumscribed by the nine-to-five workday world. Sunday is the traditional day for family gatherings, and Stafford contemplates the sorrows and the joys of family relationships. Sunday is the hiatus before the busy, quotidian concerns of life begin anew, the day "during which time one was suspended, not really waiting, hardly breathing, just suspended"; and she considers children, who watch life, awaiting

1. Jean Stafford, "Intimations of Hope," *McCall's*, XCIX (December, 1971), 77.

their chance to take part.[2] And Sunday is the loneliest day for the orphaned and the friendless, for those, displaced and dispossessed, who are denied the ability and the opportunity to participate actively in life. Stafford most poignantly views the misfit, the outcast; and for her, it is women who most clearly represent the "other" in modern society.

Jean Stafford wrote no autobiography, and relatively few of the facts of her life are known, but the information that exists presents an extremely autobiographical writer. Her uncanny understanding of children was doubtless the inheritance of her not altogether happy childhood and her youthful decision to become a writer. Her troubled romances—which commenced with a turbulent marriage to and divorce from poet Robert Lowell, followed by a second marriage and divorce, and remarriage, and ended in widowhood—accounted for her understanding of and sympathy for women alone. And her notorious hypochondria and real ill health perhaps granted her a special feeling for the exigencies of the aged and the ill. Stafford was adamant about the importance of verisimilitude in literature, and while she disliked documentary, or journalistic, fiction ("I abominate . . . the kind of writing that sets forth to tell the truth, the whole truth and nothing but the truth, with no regard to the facts that some of the truth is irrelevant, is uninteresting and can clog the works, can so embed the point in pudding that the jab of it is never felt," she wrote in "Truth in Fiction"), she pleaded the case for autobiography in fiction eloquently: "The most interesting lives of all, of course, are our own and there is nothing egotistic or unmannerly in our being keenly concerned with what happens to us. If we did not firmly believe that ours are the most absorbing experiences and the most acute perceptions and the most compelling human involvements, we would not be writers at all, and we would, as well, be very dull company."[3]

Born on July 1, 1915, in Covina, California, Jean Stafford grew up in Boulder, Colorado, which later, as the town of Adams, provided the setting for many of her stories. Her father, John Richard Stafford, who wrote western stories and a novel entitled *When Cattle Kingdom Fell* (which Stafford claimed never to have read), published under

2. Jean Stafford, "And Lots of Solid Color," *American Prefaces*, V (1939), 22.
3. Jean Stafford, "Truth in Fiction," *Library Journal*, October 1, 1966, p. 4560.

the names Jack Wonder and Ben Delight. Stafford wrote little about her family, which included two older sisters and a brother, Dick, who was killed in World War II. Her father is the delightful Dan Savage in "Woden's Day," a story extracted from her unfinished novel. A letter to her friend Peter Taylor, written in 1946 during her difficult marriage to Lowell (whose nickname was "Cal"), offers a more critical, if ambivalent, portrait of John Stafford and perhaps begins to explain Stafford's preoccupation in her fiction with fathers' relationships with their daughters. She writes about Lowell that "there was something wrong in me to marry him for he was so much like my father, whom I first worshipped and by whom I later felt betrayed."[4]

Stafford's early youth is apparently accurately portrayed in her numerous stories of childhood in Colorado. In the reminiscence "Souvenirs of Survival: The Thirties Revisited," she writes of her adolescence during the Great Depression, when she felt both guilt and pity because she was neither one of the unemployed, silent men awaiting the end of poverty and passivity, nor an "ambulatory invalid" from the local sanitarium.

From 1932 to 1936 Stafford attended the University of Colorado on a tuition scholarship supplemented with income from a summer job at a mountain dude camp (an experience that she recreates in "The Tea Time of Stouthearted Ladies") and "the best-paying undergraduate job on campus"—modeling for the life drawing class for seventy-five cents an hour (an experience that she recreates in "The Philosophy Lesson"). Stafford writes of herself and her friends, who lived at home, worked their way through school, and did not belong to the Greek-letter sororities, that "we were known as 'barbarians.'" College intellectual life consisted of gatherings in the local bar, where "several nights a week a miscellaneous handful of us used to meet to drink legal and attenuated three-point-two beer and to intoxicate ourselves, far more than the vapid brew could, with encomiums for all the writers we had just discovered—Plutarch, Joyce, Pound, Eliot, Veblen, Dostoevski, Kafka, Whitehead, Plato, Donne. . . . We had discovered how to read, and in our vernal vanity we believed we had also learned to think." "Politically illiterate," they would occasionally, from boredom, attend a Young Communist League meeting, but reck-

4. Jean Stafford to Peter Taylor, November 26, 1946, in Ian Hamilton, *Robert Lowell: A Biography* (New York, 1982), 120.

less mountaineering and beefsteak fries enlivened with rotgut whiskey offered more enticing pastimes.[5]

Graduating with a master of arts in 1936, and intrigued by the Middle Ages and medieval languages—her master's thesis was entitled "Profane and Divine Love Motifs in English Literature of the 13th Century"—Stafford won a fellowship to study philology at the University of Heidelberg and went to Europe, "the land of opportunity . . . the world, not this halfway house in which we dawdled, where the only glory and the only grandeur were what we read about." Although later "appalled by the spirit of Hitler's Germany," young Stafford was initially enchanted by Heidelberg, and the year's experience yielded some of her finest stories—"The Echo and the Nemesis," "The Maiden," "The Home Front," "A Winter's Tale," "The Cavalier," "My Blithe, Sad Bird."[6]

Stafford returned from Germany in 1937 and learned, during a year's teaching position at Stephens College in Missouri, that teaching was not to be her career. At this time, too, during her courtship with Robert Lowell, whom she had met at the University of Colorado, she suffered the serious automobile accident that cost her months in a Boston hospital, permanently marred her beauty, and inspired the story "The Interior Castle." Stafford married Lowell in 1940 and moved with him to Louisiana State University in Baton Rouge, where he studied with Cleanth Brooks and Robert Penn Warren, and she worked for a year as secretary for the *Southern Review.*

During her tempestuous and peripatetic marriage, which was characterized (as Stafford documents in "An Influx of Poets" and "A Country Love Story") by Lowell's fanatic Catholicism and her drinking and ill health, Stafford wrote and in 1944 published *Boston Adventure,* which sold some 350,000 volumes in a few months and made her enough money to finance the purchase of a long-desired house in Maine. A quiet New England life and the 1947 publication of *The Mountain Lion* were interrupted by increasing antagonism with Lowell, whose adultery spelled the end of their marriage, a termination vividly described by Stafford in "An Influx of Poets." She re-

5. Jean Stafford, "Souvenirs of Survival: The Thirties Revisited," *Mademoiselle,* L (February, 1960), 91.
    6. *Ibid.,* 175.

turned to New York and subsequently spent several months in a clinic for a "psycho-alcoholic cure."[7]

Soon after a Virgin Islands divorce (again, an experience that she captured in fiction, in "A Modest Proposal"), Stafford in 1950 married the *Life* magazine editor Oliver Jensen. The marriage was apparently a mistake, and in 1953 she was back in the Caribbean, divorcing again. During her second visit to the Virgin Islands, Stafford wrote "In the Zoo." The same year saw the publication of her first book of short stories, *Children Are Bored on Sunday*. After the 1952 publication of *The Catherine Wheel*, she turned exclusively to short fiction, which she published (forty-six stories in all), though with less frequency after the mid-1950s, until 1964, when with the appearance of the collection *Bad Characters*, she virtually stopped writing fiction.

The year 1964 also brought the death of Stafford's third husband, A. J. Liebling, who was, according to a friend, "the wise love of her life."[8] With Liebling's death Stafford retired to a quiet life on Long Island and wrote nonfiction: penetrating profiles for women's magazines of Martha Mitchell, Anne Morrow Lindbergh, Millicent Fenwick, and others; an annual Christmas roundup of children's books for the *New Yorker;* a delightful children's book of her own called *Elephi: The Cat with the High I.Q.;* an intriguing account of a three-day interview with Lee Harvey Oswald's mother, Marguerite, entitled *A Mother in History;* and assorted book reviews, satiric pieces, and essays. In 1969 Stafford chose thirty of her stories for her *Collected Stories*, which won the Pulitzer Prize the next year. Stafford, lover of cats, conversation, bourbon, and Henry James and Mark Twain, died after a long illness on March 26, 1979.

If the facts of her life exerted an influence on Stafford's work, the era in which she grew up was significant as well. Jean Stafford, born during the war whose end brought the beginning of the twentieth century and the "modern" period, was—almost inevitably—a modernist. As "Souvenirs of Survival" and many of her stories demonstrate, Stafford was keenly aware of the poverty and injustice of the Great Depression. Her fiction exhibits, too, the pervasive influence of World War II on modern society. The terrors of the war hover

7. Hamilton, *Robert Lowell*, 119.
8. Nancy Flagg, "People to Stay," *Shenandoah*, XXX (Autumn, 1979), 74.

in the background of "The Maiden," "The Captain's Gift," "The Home Front," and other stories, and war-inspired nihilism and loss of faith in human ideals reverberate throughout her stories. Unable to believe in the possibility of positive change, Stafford and her contemporaries rejected social action and embraced an art whose value lay in craftsmanship and a conservative regard for tradition. And yet, Stafford the ironist always accepted the validity of ostensibly opposite concepts, and in "The Psychological Novel," her asseveration against social novels, she qualified her rejection of "do-good books" in the statement that best presents her bleak vision of modern society.

> It is true that if we ignore the horrifying wounds of our society, we will be irresponsible, but we will be equally irresponsible if we do nothing but angrily probe them to make them hurt all the more, and we will not heal them by scolding like magpies. As human beings, and therefore as writers, we are confronted by wars and the wickedness that makes them, and the famine and disease and spiritual mutilations that follow them, by the shipwreck of our manners and our morality, by an almost universal sickness of heart. And the most romantic writers and the most diligently lighthearted clown of a writer cannot fail to be touched by the massive mood that lies upon the whole world. Still, we are not entitled to be slovenly and hysterical because the world is a mess nor to be incoherent because governments do not make sense; intolerance hardly seems the weapon most effective to fight intolerance, and fanaticism has no place in literature unless it is embodied in a character or a situation to serve a literary, not a missionary, purpose.[9]

Against the backdrop of the violence and chaos of World War II, Stafford explores the accompanying social and cultural dissolution; the questioning of liberal, humanistic ideals; the collapse of the family; the alienated individual's search for self and for communion with others, and dangerously, the alternative retreat into what Stafford calls the "interior castle" of the mind. For Stafford, as for many of her contemporaries, the complexities and horrors of the modern human condition dictated the distanced, objective stance of the ironist. Only thus removed could she present the twentieth-century human situation, the "one great incongruity, the appearance of self-valued and subjectively free but temporally finite egos in a universe that seems

9. Jean Stafford, "The Psychological Novel," *Kenyon Review*, X (Spring, 1948), 223–24.

to be utterly alien, utterly purposeless, completely deterministic, and incomprehensibly vast."[10]

Stafford's ironic vision, though a particularly appropriate response to the modern condition, was reinforced by her inheritance of the American literary tradition. American literature has from its beginnings been characterized by antithetical impulses, the innocence and naïve faith in a brave new world shadowed by the dark symbolism of the Puritan tradition. As Richard Chase illustrates, contradictions and dualities are endemic to American literature, so that as Alfred Kazin notes, by Stafford's era, "the greatest single fact about our modern American writing [was] our writers' absorption in every last detail of their American world together with their deep and subtle alienation from it."[11] Stafford inherited and merged in her work the Gothic symbolic tradition of Nathaniel Hawthorne and Herman Melville; the social criticism and novel of manners of Henry James and Edith Wharton; and the comic frontier tradition of Mark Twain and the early local colorists. Her successful manipulation of the paradoxically varied yet similar strains in American literature lends to her work a diversity and vivacity that qualify her as an important minor American writer.

Ultimately, Stafford's modernist sensibility and her American heritage are mediated by a more fundamental birthright; Stafford the ironist and Stafford the American are tempered always by Stafford the woman. If, as Judith Fetterley maintains, in a patriarchal society, "bereft, disinherited, cast out, woman is the Other, the Outsider, a mourner among children," Stafford's affinity for the lost and lonely is the peculiar sympathy of one sufferer for another, a "painful communion," a "honeymoon of cripples," a "nuptial consummation of the abandoned" (CS, 381).[12] And, I would argue, her special sympathy for the sufferers in her culture derives from her sex.

Stafford herself might disagree. Her late nonfiction prose echoes with her disapproval of the feminist movement. Pieces like "Women

10. D. C. Muecke, *Irony* (London, 1970), 68.
11. Richard L. Chase, *The American Novel and Its Tradition* (New York, 1957), 6–7; Alfred Kazin, *On Native Grounds: An Interpretation of Modern American Prose Literature* (1942; rpr. New York, 1970), ix.
12. Judith Fetterley, *The Resisting Reader: A Feminist Approach to American Fiction* (Bloomington, Ind., 1978), ix.

as Chattels, Men as Chumps" and "Don't Use Ms. with Miss Stafford, Unless You Mean ms." allowed her to sharpen her always caustic wit on Bella Abzug, Betty Friedan, and their followers in what she viewed as a trendy, somewhat absurd crusade. While she conceded, for example, that women have been and should no longer be discriminated against in the workplace, and that adequate day-care facilities and legalized abortion are reasonable, supportable notions, Stafford maintained that alimony takes unfair advantage of men and that "no legislation is going to alter" the fact that men and women are different. "To be *different*," Stafford writes, "is not to be superior or inferior; it is not bad luck that women bear and nurse the children. Just as youth is not a virtue (despite maudlin arguments to the contrary) but is a condition, so gender is neither an advantage nor an affliction but is a fact." The more lighthearted "Don't Use Ms. with Miss Stafford" protests the prevalence of the feminist abbreviation.

> Each day of my life, I set down part of an ms. since I am in the writing game, but it does not follow that I am a manuscript. I am not a Master of Science (or a Miss or a Mrs. of Science); I do not have multiple sclerosis and it would be unconscionably rude to blab the news to everybody at the P.O. if I did. You'd have mighty peculiar eye trouble if you confounded me with a motorship or a mail steamer, and you'd be nutty as a fruitcake if you mistook me for a millisecond.[13]

Indeed, Stafford inveighed against the bandwagon voguishness of "women's lib" in the 1960s and 1970s; but, a cultural conservative, and always firm about her opinions, she complained as well about plastic, the insidious effect of television on the English language, and other newfangled inventions and trends. Nonetheless, she undoubtedly would have denied the validity of feminist criticism and complained about being referred to as a woman writer. In the chapter entitled "Women's Literature" in the *Harvard Guide to Contemporary Writing*, Elizabeth Janeway defines women's literature as, not all writing by and about women, but writing that examines women's experience from within, that perceives that "women's lives run a different course from those of men" and views those lives from a distinctly feminine perspective. The very difference between men and women that Staf-

13. Jean Stafford, "Women as Chattels, Men as Chumps," New York *Times*, May 9, 1970, p. 24, and "Don't Use Ms. with Miss Stafford, Unless You Mean ms.," New York *Times*, September 21, 1973, p. 36.

ford argues for is the characteristic of her work that makes it uniquely female. As Janeway maintains, while she would exclude the work of such writers as Lillian Hellman and Mary McCarthy, whose visions are essentially masculine, "I would . . . reckon Jean Stafford as an author of women's literature while noting with respect her rejection of the tenets of the women's liberation movement."[14]

With equal respect to Jean Stafford's beliefs, I too would assert that her work can best—or at least reasonably—be read and appreciated from a feminist viewpoint. The intentional fallacy must surely be at work here; and, it can be argued, our patriarchal society's expectations of and messages to women would deter even the most liberal of women from assertions about her feminist intentions in her writing. In many ways Stafford is a conservative writer, but as Annis Pratt declares in *Archetypal Patterns in Women's Fiction:*

> Even the most conservative women authors create narratives manifesting an acute tension between what any normal human being might desire and what a woman must become. Women's fiction reflects an experience radically different from men's because our drive towards growth as persons is thwarted by our society's prescriptions concerning gender. Whether women authors are conscious of this feminism or not or force pro femina in their novels or not, or whether they are overtly concerned with being and writing about women, the tension between . . . forces demanding our submissions and our rebellious assertions of personhood, characterize far too much of our fiction to be incidental.

Other feminist critics agree that women's writing is often "palimpsestic," that its "surface designs conceal or obscure deeper, less accessible (and less socially acceptable) levels of meaning."[15]

Stafford's concern for and unique understanding of women is not hidden. The bulk of her work features female characters enacting female experiences. Ultimately, her interest is in women because they— as well as the very young and the very old—exemplify most obviously the alienation and isolation that, to some extent, all human beings feel. That women are for Stafford a metaphor for the universal

14. Elizabeth Janeway, "Women's Literature," in Daniel Hoffman (ed.), *Harvard Guide to Contemporary Writing* (Cambridge, Mass., 1979), 345.

15. Annis Pratt, *Archetypal Patterns in Women's Fiction* (Bloomington, Ind., 1981), 5–6; Sandra M. Gilbert and Susan Gubar, *The Madwoman in the Attic: The Woman Writer and the Nineteenth-Century Literary Imagination* (New Haven, 1979), 73.

condition of modern life only underscores the validity of a critical approach that seeks to illuminate her fiction from the perspective of her preoccupation with the female experience.

This is not to underestimate, however, Stafford's modernist, ironic sensibility. The "feminist" Stafford, who resents the patriarchal society's iniquities against the vulnerable and recognizes the need for change, is in contrast to the "feminine" Stafford, who, like many of her postwar contemporaries, cherishes the traditional and treasures the past. The modernist Stafford, who experiments with technical innovations in stories like "The Interior Castle," is not the conservative Stafford, who employs traditional, realistic techniques throughout most of her fiction. Louis Auchincloss, among others, contends that American women authors, as contrasted with their male colleagues, "have a sharper sense of their stake in the national heritage, and they are always at work to preserve it. They never destroy; they never want the clean sweep. They are conservatives who are always trying to conserve." Stafford concurs that "in women there is . . . the proud power to safeguard what is most worthy in the national heritage."[16]

Throughout Jean Stafford's fiction, her conflicting attitudes, her dualistic modernist and American heritage, are obvious. She asks difficult questions and offers no easy answers; she undercuts, qualifies, and contradicts. She wants to conserve, but with discrimination. Her eye is discerning, her attitude critical, and while she insists upon the preservation of traditional values, her work, often indirectly, attacks intolerance and injustice. Modernist writer, American writer, woman writer, Stafford is finally simply writer. For her the responsibility of the artist is not so much to change as to heighten awareness, to direct attention toward evil and injustice, to show the world as it really is: "Our essential problem, bad as our world is, is not different from that of serious writers at any other time in history, and this is true even in spite of the atom bomb. For the problem is how to tell the story so persuasively and vividly that our readers are taken in and are made to believe that the tale is true, that these events have happened and could happen again, and do happen everywhere and all the time."[17]

16. Louis Auchincloss, *Pioneers and Caretakers: A Study of Nine American Women Novelists* (Minneapolis, 1961), 3; Stafford, "Intimations of Hope," 77.
17. Stafford, "The Psychological Novel," 224.

In the 1940s and early 1950s, Jean Stafford was a prolific writer. Her novels were published, and her short stories—the best of which were written during these years—appeared in the *New Yorker* and other magazines with notable regularity. By the early sixties, Stafford had virtually stopped writing fiction. She continued, for the rest of her life, to publish interviews, book reviews, and witty sketches; and she was working on a novel at her death. But after 1964 Jean Stafford published only two short stories.

Except to note that during her marriage to A. J. Liebling she was happy for the first time in her life (perhaps too happy to write her typically bleak fiction), Stafford never elaborated on her curious silence, never explained the forces that impelled a serious, disciplined writer, in her middle age, to abandon her art; but there are clues. "Whenever I am asked to discuss the problems of my profession," she wrote in 1966, "I am flummoxed, because the only problem I can think of offhand is the very nearly insuperable one of writing at all. After 25 years of earning my living in this remarkably distressing way, I don't find it a bit easier than when I started out and I don't know any writer who does." The writer's worries about money and literary fashion are real, Stafford admits, but "the only way to disperse these hobgoblins is to write for yourself and God and a few close friends, and if you meet the exacting demands of this group and get their imprimatur, you can devote your whole attention to the really important agony of getting through a writing day." Perhaps the agony—exacerbated as she aged by chronic ill health, the death of her husband, and the intensifying horrors of her "improbable world"— finally overwhelmed, and silenced, Jean Stafford. "I was floundering in deep water and still am," she wrote in 1974, "forever uncertain." [18]

Stafford's fiction, at its best, captures the uncertainty and the agony of her vision. She followed her own advice, wrote for herself, God, and close friends, and as a result remains largely unread. The brittle humor in her work rests usually in clever turns of phrase and satirical characterization, and it is more often than not undercut (remember Molly Fawcett's shocking death) by her keen awareness of "the shipwreck of our manners and our morality." [19] Generally, Staf-

18. Raymond Sokolov, *Wayward Reporter: The Life of A. J. Liebling* (New York, 1980), 299; Stafford, "Truth in Fiction," 4557, 4559, and "Wordman, Spare That Tree!" *Saturday Review World*, July 13, 1974, p. 17.

19. Stafford, "The Psychological Novel," 223–24.

ford's work is characterized by unrelieved gloom. Her world is one of isolation and introspection, its inhabitants lonely, alone, searching— often in vain—for human understanding. The adept reader, the wise student of human emotions, is not put off by Stafford's sadness, for her work offers an honest, perceptive interpretation of the large horrors and small consolations of an often bleak, always complex, modern world.

I
The Company of Women
Boston Adventure

A s Jean Stafford's first, longest, and most ambitious novel, *Boston Adventure* manifests many of her characteristic themes and techniques and thus foreshadows her later work. In *Boston Adventure*, Stafford, soul mate of youth and outcasts, presents in first-person narration the story of the coming-of-age of Sonie Marburg, the only daughter of poor European immigrants, whose single desire is to escape the squalor of her home in a Massachusetts fishing village for nearby Boston, which in her romanticized fantasy is symbolized by the candescent glitter of the Boston State House dome.

Abandoned early in the novel by her loving but feckless father, Sonie undertakes her journey toward adulthood with an assortment of women who present a variety of life-styles and models for female adult behavior. Through these characters, major and minor, and Sonie's interactions with them, Jean Stafford examines the female role in society and women's reactions, both conscious and unconscious, to their situations. In this novel of female development, Stafford presents an intelligent, sensitive young woman confronted with the options that women have—and are denied—in an essentially patriarchal society, and demonstrates her interest in the lives of women in modern American culture.

Contemporary feminist critics have noted that the traditional definition of the novel of development, or *Bildungsroman*, presumes a male protagonist and his struggle to learn to function in a male world. Yet these same critics have rediscovered an impressive number of novels—*Jane Eyre, Madame Bovary, Mrs. Dalloway, The Awakening, The Mill on the Floss, Little Women*—that trace the development of a young female protagonist or the awakening of a mature woman character. And with the recent awareness in women's fiction and women's lives of the need for the conscious creation of a self, feminist critics maintain, the female *Bildungsroman* is a viable and vital literary form. Ellen Morgan writes that "the female bildungsroman appears to be becoming the most salient form for literature influenced by neo-feminism. The novel of apprenticeship is admirably suited to express the emergence of women from cultural conditioning into struggle with institutional forces, their progress toward the goal of full personhood, the effort to restructure their lives and society according to their own vision of meaning and right living."[1]

Contemporary women authors can create their novels of development with an appreciation of the tradition of the female *Bildungsroman* and a new awareness of the opportunities and limitations that their young protagonists encounter. Yet earlier female novelists did not simply put Wilhelm Meister in a dress. The female novel of formation traditionally culminates in a vision of a world far removed from the active social milieu that the young male hero commonly comes to understand and occupy. For the youthful female hero, adulthood means a mitigation of intellectual activity or a mandate to marry and have children, and often results in a rejection of society's restrictions that manifests itself in death or a withdrawal to the "interior castle" of the mind. As Morgan maintains: "The female protagonists who did grow as selves were generally halted and defeated before they reached transcendent selfhood. They committed suicide or died; they compromised by marrying and devoting themselves to sympathetic men; they went mad or into some kind of retreat and seclusion from the world. They grew up to a point, and then . . . they 'grew down.'"[2] The female *Bildungsroman*, then, is traditionally a tale of compromise

1. Ellen Morgan, "Humanbecoming: Form and Focus in the Neo-Feminist Novel," in Susan Koppelman Cornillon (ed.), *Images of Women in Fiction: Feminist Perspectives* (Bowling Green, 1972), 185.
2. *Ibid.*, 184.

and disillusionment, the chronicle of a young woman's recognition that, for her, life offers not limitless possibilities but an unsympathetic environment in which she must struggle to discover a room of her own. In *Boston Adventure*, Jean Stafford echoes the notes of disappointment that her foremothers sounded, and her music is contrapuntal and cacophonous. With her inevitable rejection of easy answers, Stafford takes Sonie on a journey filled with surprises and ambiguities and to an adulthood that is neither completely satisfactory nor without validity.

The earliest, most fundamental bond is with the mother, who is, for the female, the first and strongest role model; but Stafford presents Sonie with a female parent whose personality and circumstances make her unacceptable as a model for mature behavior. Shura Korf Marburg seems the perfect mother, a manifestation of the quintessential mother figure, the Virgin Mary—she is a "madonna" to her doctor and the gardener; Sonie describes her as a "holy" beauty; and, claim the residents of the Hotel Barstow, where she works as a chambermaid, she is "the image of a saint" (*BA*, 50). But Shura's elegant beauty belies the bitter misery of her life.

Disappointed by Herman Marburg's inability to fulfill his courtship promises of luxury and happiness in America, Shura nightly excoriates her miserable husband as a failure and narrates the story of her childhood for him and Sonie, whose presence in her parents' room makes her the reluctant audience for their incessant nocturnal agonies. It is a narrative of cold, hunger, and parental abuse. "It was a tale so fantastic that not even I, a little girl, could believe it," Sonie writes. "Yet it was so horrible that to scoff at it would have been inhuman" (*BA*, 7).

After her mother's death, Shura's grief-stricken, drunken father maligns his dead wife and casts ten-year-old Shura and her siblings into the cold of a Moscow January night. Shura finds refuge with Luibka, a "witch" who mutilates men who want to avoid military service. She is not a bad woman, Shura claims, but "the innocent slave of the wicked men who patronized her" (*BA*, 9). Luibka is kind to the homeless girl who serves as her maid, but the abuse that Shura suffers from the male customers and the violence of her benefactor's profession send her eventually to a new position. Working as a waitress at an officer's tavern, Shura, now fourteen and beautiful, is repulsed by the men's overt advances and, when she rebuffs them, their physical abuse. At seventeen she sails for America and meets and marries Herman Marburg, whose failure to live up to his pledges only reinforces her distrust of and aversion to men.

Tall, sensual Shura, rejected by her father and disappointed by her husband, blames all men for her misery. With the weapon of her tireless voice, she harangues Marburg, whose failure in business is exacerbated by his alienation from his Catholic religion, until, desperate and demoralized, he abandons twelve-year-old Sonie and his pregnant wife. She bears a boy, Ivan, and though Sonie instinctively feels love for the scrawny, ugly infant, Shura views her son as the curse of his absent father. She ignores Ivan, leaving Sonie and neighbors to care for him. As Ivan grows, Shura slips into her own irrational world, her indifference changing to the loathing that drives the boy to his death.

Sonie is perplexed by her mother's antipathy toward Ivan until, finally, she understands that for her mother, men are the embodiment of evil: "I had known that . . . she had hated my brother and, later, throughout his lifetime, I had sometimes wondered why she had not hated him as she had carried him before his birth and why she had not hated me. She had not, because she had fortified herself long, long before, with the conviction that all men were villains and women were their innocent victims" (*BA*, 153).

After Ivan's death, Shura's encroaching madness is aggravated by nightmares about her son and a lingering influenza that subjects her once again to the presence of a loathed male, the florid, dipsomaniacal Dr. Galbraith, who brings flowers with his medicine and invites Shura to recuperate at his mountain cabin. Shura's delayed but violent reaction to the doctor's advances is the final stage in her descent into madness, and Sonie finally grudgingly admits that her mother must be hospitalized. Incarcerated in a sanitarium, a move that accords Sonie the freedom to pursue her dream of a life in Boston with Miss Pride, Shura is originally diagnosed as manic depressive. When she later exhibits symptoms of catatonia, and the sanitarium doctor informs Sonie that she can no longer visit her mother, Shura disappears from the novel—and, it seems, from Sonie's life as well.

It is difficult not to view Shura as the villain of *Boston Adventure*. Irascible and misanthropic, she persecutes not only her pitiable husband and defenseless son but often the innocent neighbors as well. She cares for Sonie, but eventually, as her hold on reality weakens, she rejects her daughter too, and turning on Sonie, she hisses, "I hate you" (*BA*, 216). As a narrator, Sonie (and, at least to an extent, Stafford) is hard on Shura, who is lazy, egocentric, slovenly, and moody. But a traditional—that is to say, male—interpretation of Shura as virago, as evil and crazy, underestimates her complexity as a character and as a woman, for in many ways Shura is a victim. The violence of her childhood and adolescence leaves emotional scars, and her escape to America brings, not the happy, affluent life that Herman Marburg promises on the ship that brings the young immigrants to their new home, but more poverty and privation.

None of Shura's behavior is more reprehensible yet more indicative of her unhappiness and confusion than that characterizing her relationship with her son. Ivan is for Shura a living monument to his repugnant father and to all men. Sensing his mother's antipathy, the boy grows up to be, in Shura's words, a "little black beast of a boy" (*BA*, 112). His virulent epileptic fits disgust Shura and the neighbors, and even Sonie believes that "he was a beast, the very repository of bestiality, composed of filth and evil, as though his interior life, in the cavern of that rocking skull, were one of utter nastiness" (*BA*, 117). Evil like his mother, victim like his mother, five-year-old Ivan, apparently no match for his mother's loathing, dies after he flees into a snowstorm from her powerful penetrating eyes. But finally, as his appearances in Shura's dreams hasten her journey toward insanity, the male child triumphs over the woman. Sonie blames her mother for Ivan's death; she believes that Shura's nightmares are her punishment, but she recognizes, too, that the woman's soft cry of "I tried!" when she learns of the boy's death means that she had tried to love him (*BA*, 128).

Rejected by her father, abandoned by her husband, denied the presence of her mother and the ability to love her son, Shura Marburg is a frustrated, tortured woman. She is poor, without skills, lonely, and homesick for her native land. After Marburg's sudden exodus, Sonie hopes that Shura will no longer spend all her time staring at the sea. She states that while "my father from his [shop] windows, and I from Miss Pride's [at the Hotel], looked toward Boston . . . my mother, looking out the windows of our kitchen, could see only a long white stretch of sand and a few crags far off, and then the endless sea itself. It was an arresting landscape but one whose monotony became maddening in time" (*BA*, 56). Maddening indeed. Sonie's youthful imperceptiveness is never more apparent than when she maintains that toward the "sameness" of her view Shura "was altogether indifferent" (*BA*, 56). Shura has no hopes, no chance, as Sonie does, for escape from her "stifling little box of a life"—no escape, that is, except the one that women have always had, an escape within, to physical and mental illness (*BA*, 5).

Always difficult and eccentric, Shura exhibits increasingly irrational behavior when Marburg disappears. When she and Sonie are more than ever in need of money she quits her job at the Hotel, where she has been offered a raise, because she cannot bear to face her neighbors. For years she clings stubbornly to the illusion that the "golden egg," fifty dollars that Sonie has gotten for Marburg's old ski equipment, will provide for the family. During Ivan's short life, his mother never leaves their two-room cottage. She devotes herself with almost comical assiduity to her embroidery of colorful birds—peacocks, parrots, and bluebirds are her favorites—never recognizing that her exquisite creatures are lacking their tail feathers.

Like her creations, Shura is a beautiful bird who cannot fly, and is thus a stereotypical figure in women's fiction. Discussing what she calls "the enclosure archetype" in women's writing, Annis Pratt states that women writers create "their most complex embellishments" on the archetype in their mad wives. Pratt notes Phyllis Chesler's assertion in her book *Women and Madness* that incarceration and madness are "both an expression of female powerlessness and an unsuccessful attempt to reject and overcome this fate. Madness and asylums generally function as mirror images of the female experience, and as penalties for being 'female,' as well as for daring not to be."[3]

Early in *Boston Adventure* Sonie walks home after her first conversation with Nathan Kadish, the boy next door who is to become her first boyfriend, and, with typical Staffordian irony, in her happiness sings one of her mother's songs, a song about women and courtship that ends thus:

3. Pratt, *Archetypal Patterns in Women's Fiction*, 51, 34.

Night came down upon the stubble.
Women have all kinds of trouble!
Woman's sad lot! Oh,
Woman's sad lot! (*BA*, 77)

Sonie loves her mother and cares for her as long as Shura needs her. But Shura's life is a failure, and the girl recognizes early on that her mother offers no model for a mature and acceptable adulthood. "Who do you love, little Sonie girl?" her mother asks early in the novel, and young but confident Sonie remarks, "While I answered as she desired me to, my mind was telling me the truth: 'Miss Pride, not you, Mamma'" (*BA*, 28).

In her examination of the lives of very young and very old women, Stafford again works within a female literary tradition. Within the spectrum of women's fiction, writes Annis Pratt, women exist who reject society's expectations—"young women not yet enclosed, on the one hand, and older women beyond bothering with the domestic enclosure, on the other. For the woman past her 'prime,' as for the young hero not yet approaching hers, visions of authenticity come more easily than to women in the midst of their social experience."[4] In such stories as "Life Is No Abyss," "The Bleeding Heart," and "My Blithe, Sad Bird," the young, usually female protagonist experiences a dramatic, often painful revelation about life as a result of her relationship with an aging woman. In Lucy Pride of *Boston Adventure*, Stafford presents her variation on the archetype of the mentor, the Jungian "wise old man" who is so often in women's writing an astute old woman, and allows Sonie a vision of a life far removed from her mother's. For if in Shura Marburg Stafford explores the effects of marriage and disillusionment on the adult woman, in Lucy Pride she creates a single, independent woman whose age and social status make her a dramatically different model for Sonie. And, as always, the character and Stafford's attitude toward her are complex and ambivalent.

Sonie's attraction to Lucy Pride develops early in her life, well before *Boston Adventure* begins. The novel opens with Sonie's assertion that "because we were very poor and could not buy another bed, I

4. *Ibid.*, 11.

used to sleep on a pallet made of old coats and comforters in the same room with my mother and father. When I played wishing games or said 'Star light, star bright,' my first wish always was that I might have a room of my own, and the one I imagined was Miss Pride's at the Hotel Barstow which I sometimes had to clean when my mother, the chambermaid, was not feeling well" (*BA*, 3).

Around Miss Pride and her room, from the windows of which she can see Boston and its State House dome, Sonie constructs an elaborate fantasy of a life with the woman she adores, a fantasy into which she escapes from the horrors of her life in Chichester. Early in the novel, after Shura's agonizing repetition of the sordid story of her childhood in Russia and yet another argument with her miserable husband, she cautions Marburg to be quiet so that he won't awaken Sonie, and the frustrated father whispers, "The child should never have been born." Sonie, feigning sleep while her parents fight, reacts to her father's painful pronouncement.

> Over and over, until my eyes closed, I imagined the day on which my parents would die and Miss Pride would come and take me to live at the Hotel, if they died in the summer, or in Boston, if in the winter. Or I watched the waves part and saw a dry path laid for me between the water's furniture and then I stepped forward off the beach and walked across to the first wharf in Boston harbor. I could hear their undertone, gentle and melancholy, reiterating endlessly my father's words: the child should never have been born. (*BA*, 10–11)

Lucy Pride and Boston symbolize for Sonie all that her life in Chichester lacks—culture, comfort, stability. A staid Beacon Hill aristocrat, Miss Pride summers in the small nearby fishing village where the Marburgs live and work. There are other elderly summer residents at the Barstow, but though the proper Miss Pride is cordial to her compatriots, she is quite obviously unlike them. While the others express their preoccupation with the weather, Lucy Pride, dressed at all times in a black broadcloth suit and a beaver hat, "apparently suffered neither from the heat nor from the cold, for she did not shiver or perspire, and she was never heard to discuss the temperature" (*BA*, 13–14).

As Miss Pride, "straight as a gun-barrel," takes her morning constitutional on the beach, Sonie, working as a chambermaid while her mother is ill, admires "her immaculate attire and her proud carriage" from the window of the old woman's room (*BA*, 14). The other women inhabit messy bedrooms strewn with soiled clothes and spilled cosmetics and medicine, but "in Miss Pride's room, there was never anything amiss" (*BA*, 15). Sonie lingers lovingly over her hero's accoutrements—the spotless white silk gloves, the jewelry, the desk accessories. "Though I touched nothing," she remembers, "I took in everything" (*BA*, 16).

An observant narrator, Sonie does notice much about Miss Pride, though hardly everything. She is ten years old as the novel begins, and blind with adoration for the old-fashioned, pragmatic Bostonian; and while she recognizes the inherent attractions of Miss Pride's cultured personality and life-style, she is too naïve to understand that her longing to live with Lucy Pride is in large measure a desire to escape the tribulations of her own life. The dissimilarities between their worlds are notable. Miss Pride's room, in its neatness, contrasts markedly with the Marburgs' cottage, where Sonie sleeps on a pile of old coats and blankets, and eats in a kitchen that has a cheese box for a footstool and bookshelves crowded with tools, seashells, and assorted junk. Miss Pride, in her tailored black suit, bears little resemblance to the "shaggy," unkempt Marburg and his sensually slovenly wife in her bright, flowing garb. Physically and emotionally, Sonie's world is chaotic and unnerving; her attraction to the self-contained, poised Lucy Pride is virtually inevitable.

Miss Pride's appeal for Sonie extends beyond her fastidious, fine manners. "Because we were very poor," *Boston Adventure* begins, and as Sonie listens to her parents' incessant arguments about unkept promises and unfulfilled dreams, she arrives at the conclusion that the lack of money is responsible for their misery. Again substituting for Shura at the Hotel, as she serves lunch to Miss Pride and her lawyer, she listens in awe to their discussions of taxes and dividends (*BA*, 93). A sensitive and intelligent girl, Sonie is attracted too by Lucy Pride's learning and culture. "Even more than her familiarity with high finance," she writes, "I was stirred by her intellectual life" (*BA*, 93). Sonie is impressed that whereas she, when involved in a book, reads for hours at a time, Miss Pride devotes two disciplined hours a day to her perusal of the *Atlantic Monthly, Harper's Magazine*, and the novels of Anthony Trollope, Henry James, William Makepeace Thackeray, and William Dean Howells.

So, throughout her childhood and adolescence, Sonie dreams about the wealthy, sophisticated Lucy Pride, who is, in her own words, "the most old-fashioned woman in Boston," and about the mysterious, seductive city that is an essential component of the old woman's charm (*BA*, 158). When Miss Pride, upon learning that Herman Marburg is an educated artisan, engages him to make shoes for her and her niece, Hopestill, Sonie escapes in the refuge of her dreams her shame that the Marburg family remains merely hired help to the woman: "My reveries of life in Boston persisted, became, indeed, as my experience widened, more specific and in a sense more real than my existence in Chichester" (*BA*, 30). Chichester, though, is all too real. Marburg's desertion leaves Sonie with the responsibilities of caring for her increasingly anomalous mother and recalcitrant brother, and she fulfills her duties with the occasional but requisite solace of her fantasy. "Although the years had brought me new and sometimes strong infatuations, knowledge had not abused the dream of my childhood," she remarks. "My perspective of all else might have changed, but Miss Pride and Miss Pride's room had remained unaltered, so that even now, when I was no longer a child, I had often in the summer time been healed of my anxieties over Ivan and Mamma the moment I stepped across the threshold of the room" (*BA*, 108).

No wonder, then, that even an older, more perceptive Sonie cannot risk an impairment of her image of her hero. When at eighteen she is confronted with her inability to provide a funeral for Ivan, she turns to the only representative of stability that she has ever known, promising in return for the money to bury her small brother, "my services in the humblest part of her establishment for the rest of my life" (*BA*, 134). Bearing condolences and a potted plant, Miss Pride arrives, but a day too late, and Sonie for the first time sees not the "grand Bostonian to whose slightest favor I had aspired" but a selfish, repulsive old woman. The recognition is alarming, and, threatened, Sonie represses it: "A censor in me checked me before I had disarrayed her features beyond repair, and as from her small, brisk person there emanated the sharp odor of her expensive soap, she recovered her familiar and beloved shape" (*BA*, 154).

As though aware of the momentary wavering of Sonie's adoration, but more likely from guilt at her delayed action, Lucy Pride invites the bereaved girl to tea at her home on Pinckney Street, explaining

with characteristic candor that her invitation and her interest in
Sonie result from her perception that since Sonie, neither servant nor
aristocrat, belongs to a class—the artisan class—that no longer exists
in America, the girl must "skip a grade" (*BA*, 159). Neither at this
time nor later, when she offers Sonie a position as her personal secretary, does she make clear whether her young protégée is to move forward or backward on the social scale; and Sonie, despite her mentor's
revealing pronouncements about her refusal to change and her rever-
ence for the past, is too preoccupied with her long-awaited visit to
revered Boston to be concerned about her status in the old woman's
house. But the event, predictably, fails to fulfill her expectations.
As the car passes through bleak, noisy slums, Sonie, surprised that
she cannot see the State House dome, asks Miss Pride whether they
will drive past it. "'Oh, you shall see it, never fear. I see you've been
properly brought up to respect Boston.' Her voice was ironic. 'But I'll
let you in on a secret—I think the State House is a perfect fright'"
(*BA*, 162).

The scene is portentous. Sonie's first view of Boston proffers a city
completely different from the sanctum she has cultivated in her imagination for nearly ten years. Only much later in the novel does Sonie
recognize that its "merry slums" and "murderous children" are metaphors for the hypocritical, depraved society into which Miss Pride
will soon introduce her innocent friend (*BA*, 161). Perhaps more im-
portantly, the scene highlights the innate differences between Sonie
and Lucy Pride. The old woman ironically disparages Sonie's sincere
respect for Boston and fails to recognize the grandeur and beauty of
the dome that is so stirring to her protégée. Significantly, too, although she recognizes that her romantic attachment to the dome has
been attenuated by Miss Pride's failure to appreciate its grandeur,
Sonie does not see that she is prepared to compromise her dream in
order to accommodate her sacred adulation of Miss Pride. Soon after
Sonie states that she is "dashed" by Miss Pride's contempt for the
State House, she notes that as "we walked to her house down the
street past the State House to which I found myself indifferent . . . at
the moment I released my long-cherished impression of it, I realized
that my desire for Boston had never been so real as it was now as,
grimy, tattered, large for my age, I strode beside this clean, tart
woman, so certain of her good blood, her wit, her wealth, her position

in society . . . that she could appear on the streets of her city in any company without the slightest risk of censure" (*BA*, 163). Sonie's negative self-image aside, the salient fact is that she resents neither Miss Pride's patronizing charity nor her unconscious but insensitive deflation of the important symbol.

Shura's deteriorating health distracts Sonie for a time from her new relationship with Miss Pride, but when Dr. Galbraith suddenly dies, she uses her friendship with the old woman to arrange an appointment with Hopestill's beau, Dr. Philip McAllister. After Shura is hospitalized, the doctor accompanies Sonie on her visits to the sanitarium. When, at the end of the summer and her job at the Hotel, he asks Sonie about her plans, she reaffirms her desire to serve Lucy Pride "as her housemaid or her laundress or her lady-in-waiting" (*BA*, 225). But when Philip suggests that the position as Miss Pride's secretary may be more appropriate for Sonie, she reacts with ambivalence: "I was not so pleased as I felt I should have been. . . . I was invaded by the same doubt of her that I had felt . . . after Ivan's death and I had seen her in the winter sunlight for the briefest moment as an old, ugly woman inspired by a tenuous and urbane evil" (*BA*, 225). This time Sonie need not tell us that she cannot allow herself to "disarray" her devotion to Lucy Pride. She cannot envision a life beyond Boston; given her background, her innocence, her social restrictions, and her sex, the only life Sonie can imagine is to serve Miss Pride. And she can ensure her contentment with her fate only if she refuses to acknowledge its limitations.

Sonie is therefore happy when she begins her long-awaited life on Pinckney Street with Lucy Pride and her own room, even though Miss Pride does not hesitate to instruct her young friend in the proprieties of her position. When Miss Pride decides that Sonie is ready to be introduced to Boston society, Sonie perceives the ambiguity of her position. Neither servant, secretary, nor companion, she is Miss Pride's "'case' or her 'project' or whatever the word was that was then in fashion to describe the beneficiary of that allotment in a rich woman's budget called 'Miscellany'" (*BA*, 238). Sonie is to study at business college until Miss Pride is prepared to begin her memoirs, and like the ingenue actress in a hundred old movies, "[her] background was to be obliterated from [her] memory" (*BA*, 238). Miss Pride, who fears old age and senility, recognizes Sonie as a potential "caretaker," and when she asks the girl—with the implication that Sonie will be remembered in her will—to consider staying at Pinckney Street forever, Sonie is "grateful and happy at the prospect" (*BA*, 238). Later, thinking of Nathan's romantic plans to live and write in Paris, she reaffirms her commitment to her new life-style.

> When I had promised myself . . . that I would have the best, I had allowed destiny to choose the circumstances for me. I had at no time doubted that the choice of Boston by my guardian angel had been supreme wisdom, that this was the soil in which my gifts, whatever they were, would fructify. . . . My talents were not artistic, not creative. I felt that they were assimilative and analytical, that what I saw in Boston, what I had seen in Chichester I understood, but that I could not reassemble my impressions into something artful. I could not ennoble fact. It was experience of the most complex order that I desired, and while there were times when . . . I wished my knowledge to include the cafés and *ateliers* and the quays of . . . Paris, the wish was diluted as I . . . thought of my room, of Miss Pride, and of our conversation over the sherry glasses. She, I thought, was worth all the freedom and all the abandon, worth, indeed, all triumphs. (*BA*, 240)

Sonie's rejection of the life that Nathan offers occurs at the beginning of Book Two, before she enters the social milieu that Miss Pride and her niece represent. Her new life introduces her to complex experience indeed, and as she comes to know the upright Bostonians who have appended to their Puritan ancestors' stern morality their own modern prejudices and "blue-blooded ugliness," she understands increasingly the ignoble reality of the aristocratic society and the vulnerability of her employer (*BA*, 250). When Miss Pride expresses her annoyance at Sonie's friendship with Philip McAllister, which she dislikes not only because he is Hopestill's boyfriend but because he is above Sonie's class, the girl recognizes for the first time the strength of her position. "I don't want you to drift away from me," Miss Pride complains, and while Sonie assures the old woman that she intends to remain on Pinckney Street, she recognizes that her power arises from Miss Pride's insecurity. As Miss Pride ages, Sonie fears, her demands might become increasingly burdensome, and the girl resolves privately to maintain her freedom. Yet, as ever, Stafford obfuscates the situation, and Sonie's awareness of Miss Pride's reliance on her is mitigated by her recognition of her lack of choices. "I had got my wish," she notes, "and could find no other" (*BA*, 315).

As Sonie continues to observe, and becomes increasingly involved in, Miss Pride's milieu and Hopestill's tragedy, her insight into the hypocrisies of her environment deepens.[5] Yet, as Sonie's knowledge of her mentor grows, so too does her appreciation of the old woman's strength and old-fashioned values. "Miss Pride," she writes, "no matter what scandals and disasters were perpetrated under her very nose, would never change. . . . So long as Miss Pride was here, I thought, I could face anything" (*BA*, 461). Again, however, Stafford forbids facile alternatives: it is not Sonie's admiration for Lucy Pride's character that elicits her final commitment. When Shura begins to exhibit signs of recovery and the doctors suggest that she may be released from the sanitarium, Sonie once again has only Miss Pride to appeal to for help, and with her request she sacrifices her control of her situation. The old woman promises to provide for Sonie's mother, but her price is high: "She extended her old claw to me. 'Agree!' she cried. 'Agree never to leave me until I die!' She smiled, but the terror of death was in her yellow eyes and in her voice, and . . . my whole soul retreated from her in the appalled vision of her awful dependence, her hideous cowardice. 'Agree!' she was crying. 'I agree,' I said, but my voice was unnatural" (*BA*, 481). Sonie muses upon her situation on her journey to the hospital: "My double servitude, that to my mother and to Miss Pride, lay heavy on me, and now . . . the die was cast. I could not, morally, disappear. Just before we reached the asylum, I regained control of myself, said I loved my mother and I loved Miss Pride and Boston and that nothing could ever shake me from my resolve to live the rest of my life exactly as I was living it now" (*BA*, 481). Moments later, only hours after her commitment to remain with Miss Pride, Sonie learns that her mother will not need alternative care—will, in fact, never recover from her illness.

Sonie is a sympathetic character in a moral novel, and as *Boston Adventure* ends, there is no question that she will honor her pledge to remain with the aging Lucy Pride until her death. And yet, Jean Stafford will not allow such an uncomplicated denouement. If Sonie is morally obligated to her benefactor, she is also psychologically and

5. Stafford's keen observation of Boston society was undoubtedly facilitated by her introduction into the life of the aristocratic Lowell family. Her in-laws, especially Robert Lowell's mother, Charlotte, were unimpressed with their son's wife, and Stafford, like Sonie, was alienated from their pretentious world.

socially incapable of choosing any other course of action. The traditional *Bildungsroman* typically chronicles the integration of the young hero into a social environment, and while the quest of the middle-aged female protagonist in women's fiction is often spiritual, the female *Bildungsroman* typically echoes the social concerns of the male prototype. The difference is not in the quest but in its outcome. The purpose of the novel of development is, for the female hero, "frequently aborted by society's unwillingness to assimilate her."[6]

In *Boston Adventure*, more than in any of her later fiction, Stafford explores society and her characters' lives within it. She concentrates on two environments that seem to share only geographical proximity. The novel is divided into two nearly equal parts, a structure that provides a paradigm for the dichotomies of the novel. Whereas in Book One, "Hotel Barstow," Shura is for Sonie the central figure, in Book Two, "Pinckney Street," Lucy Pride functions as the symbol of the aristocratic urban society that Sonie envisions as her escape from her squalid, restrictive life in Chichester. So limited are Sonie's experience and opportunities that she can imagine only one alternative to the disordered, unsatisfactory life that her mad mother represents. Yet, when she finally moves to the ostensibly civilized Boston, the society about which Miss Pride asserts, "*We* know the real thing," Sonie discovers that the irrationalities of her life in Chichester are supplanted by a more subtle, pervasive, and conscious compulsion to camouflage reality (*BA*, 26). Soon after the girl's arrival in Boston, Hopestill, with unwitting accuracy, confronts her with the question: "Are you somebody incognito? As they say, scratch a Russian waitress and you find an archduchess. I suppose it works the other way too, scratch an archduchess and you find an upstairs maid" (*BA*, 276). Gradually, we learn that subterfuge and concealment are common in this society. Lucy Pride, therefore, though her age and her money render her immune from her culture's disapprobation, is, as the representative of her society, as confining to Sonie as is her mother.

While Shura Marburg and Lucy Pride differ in virtually every aspect of their personalities and lives, they share an intrinsic aversion to men. Yet even in their affinity the women diverge, for though Shura's misandry is overt and virulent, Lucy Pride's more fearful an-

6. Pratt, *Archetypal Patterns in Women's Fiction*, 136.

tipathy is obfuscated. Certainly Miss Pride's single status appeals to Sonie. In an early childhood fantasy, as blond Antoinette de la Mar, Sonie rejects her numerous suitors: "She had already decided not to marry anybody . . . she lived only for Miss Pride who adored her" (*BA*, 31). And although Shura "for so many years and so diligently had schooled me in the treacheries of men," Sonie writes, her intention to remain single is "more in imitation of Miss Pride than to escape the pitfalls my mother had described to me" (*BA*, 76).

Intransigently traditional, Lucy Pride, though she claims to be "an advocate of equal rights," is no feminist (*BA*, 167). "Braininess," she maintains, is useless to a woman, and learning is "a masculine province" (*BA*, 158). She idolizes her deceased father, indeed, preserves his library in his memory; and although her aged friend Admiral Nephews implies vaguely that he once courted Lucy Pride, the independent, aloof old woman is clearly a virgin. She is, in fact, as Sonie comes to recognize, almost hermaphroditic. When entertaining, she maintains the traditional division of the party; the men retire to the library for whiskey and brandy while the ladies enjoy Cointreau in the drawing room, and Lucy Pride, "being without a master for her parties, played both roles" (*BA*, 235). Sonie wonders what has "disguised her feminine nature so that the bequests of her male ancestors were more apparent than those handed down from the mothers of her line" (*BA*, 265). And finally, late in the novel, by now integrally involved in the lives of Miss Pride, Hopestill, and their associates, Sonie experiences an epiphanic revelation: "I had gone too far, by becoming myself a protagonist, to believe blindly any longer that Miss Pride's was the ideal pattern: there was, in the tone of her voice, cold and neutral, a suggestion of ingrown, conceited lewdness which, having no sexuality to modify, advertised the secret nudity of the old, arid carcass" (*BA*, 359).

Lucy Pride's attitudes toward sex are symbolized in the novel in her relationship with her cat. Only late in the novel does Sonie discover that Miss Pride has a pet, and when Hopestill mentions Mercy, Sonie feels that "there was something perplexing and a little unpleasant in [Miss Pride's] concealment of it" (*BA*, 275). Sonie learns that Mercy, petulant after the destruction of her litter of kittens, is immured in an upstairs bedroom. Although she recognizes the sad similarity between her fate and the animal's, it is Hopestill who forces her to confront the resemblance.

> Listen to me, you child, you baby, you innocent little girl: the time will
> come when you will see through that woman and know her for the bitch
> she is. It's that she's got to have power. . . . As soon as Aunt Lucy saw
> that she couldn't control me . . . she got a cat! . . . Oh, she fed Mercy
> well . . . and every now and again . . . [she] was allowed to come down
> and purr for Aunt Sarah and Uncle Arthur and Admiral Nephews. Un-
> til, mind you, she had a chance to perpetuate her species and have four
> hybrid kittens and then she was permanently incarcerated. . . . But a
> pussy-cat wasn't enough, and now she's got *you*, and she intends to have
> the time of her life with you because you're helpless. You're dependent
> on her. (*BA*, 446)

Sonie *is* dependent upon Lucy Pride. And just as her dissatisfaction
with her life at home sent her to Boston, though her lack of alternatives and her commitment to the old woman keep her on Pinckney
Street, her disquietude prods her to flee Miss Pride's room for another.

Stafford introduces the room motif in the second sentence of *Boston Adventure*, when Sonie identifies her single wish as a room of her
own. A room of one's own is a sanctuary, a heterocosm. It is, as well,
reflective of its owner's personality. Sonie's childhood friend Betty
Brunson's bedroom, for example, is furnished with porcelain shep-
herdess lamps, movie star photographs, and other trappings that betray her childishness and her family's bourgeois ostentation. Miss
Pride's room at the Hotel is, like its occupant, the image of order. The
Pinckney Street drawing room, concordant with Miss Pride's respect
for the past, is furnished exactly as it has been for generations.

Her move to Boston brings Sonie a room of her own, and, she observes, "the joy that my room gave me was . . . so intense that my
being required its articulation and sometimes I could not see the deep
mole-colored carpet and the silvery draperies at the windows for my
tears" (*BA*, 236). Yet, gradually, inevitably, Sonie recognizes that no
physical room is sufficient refuge from Miss Pride's rapacious grasp
on her life. After a difficult scene with the old woman, she flees to her
room, stands at the window, and "automatically, I said, 'Star light,
star bright. . . .' But I had got my wish and could find no other. The
room was here and my signature was on it: my own pajamas and dark
blue wrapper would be lying on the turned-down bed" (*BA*, 315–16).
Like her mother's, now Sonie's only avenue of escape is internal.

Sonie unwittingly introduces the interior-castle theme early in the
novel, when, describing her reaction to her parents' nocturnal dis-
cord, she writes that "I was propelled by their curses into conscious-

ness and seemed driven into a socket in the dark from which there was no outlet. My bounded brain was as inalterable as a ball and it could neither veer in flight nor proceed to understanding: solid and of one material, terror, it lay in a minute cavern whose walls were fashioned from the rhetoric and the darkness" (*BA*, 33). Many years later, burdened with her mother's illness and the news of Hopestill's pregnancy and engagement to Philip, Sonie finds asylum, appropriately, while visiting her mother in the sanitarium. In the "cataleptic tranquillity" of the hospital common room, she relaxes and begins to daydream. Suddenly there appears "a single, clear-cut image which could not be worried into any sort of relationship with what had gone before. Irrelevant, impulsively independent, there was before my eyes a room which I had never seen, but a room in which there was hardly an object that was unfamiliar. It was possible that I had fallen asleep and had dreamed of such a place, and yet it did not fade upon my scrutiny of it, but, static, pictorial, it was present to me like a projection on a screen" (*BA*, 391). Shabby and shadowy, the room overlooks a court surrounded by cluttered balconies; its windows reflect a red, autumnal sunset. It contains, besides ponderous, dark furniture, a small table, a Victorian writing desk, French and German books. Sonie analyzes the vision.

> I reviewed the rooms in which I had been, as far back as I could remember, but I could not place it, and while, as I have said, it was by no means unfamiliar and all the objects were as real as if I had owned them for many years, I could not, nevertheless, actually identify any of them. I cannot say how long the "vision" of this red room lasted, but while it did, I experienced a happiness, a removal from the world which was not an escape so much as it was a practiced unworldliness. And it was a removal which was also a return. The happiness was not unmixed: as I gazed at the red evening sunlight through the brick chimneys of the court, I was filled with a tranquil mortal melancholy as if I were out of touch with the sources of experience so that I could receive but could not participate; that is, I could *assume* the boys were shouting in the street, but I could not hear them. (*BA*, 392)

Shura's sudden cry, "I'm in the crazy house!" jolts Sonie back into reality with the renewed awareness that she is responsible for her mother's confinement (*BA*, 393). Later, when the doctor informs her that Shura may be recovering, she feels, besides guilt, sudden terror at the prospect of again caring for the ill woman, and fear that she

herself may be going insane. Sonie closes her eyes to shut out the doctor and "seemed to descend once more through the wide, moving air
and then, purged, absolved, emptied of all that did not pertain to solitude, I saw the red room with its wedges of shadow, its prospect of
eternally slumbering cats. When, with the opening of my eyes, the
room disappeared, I thought of adding to my list of suspicions about
myself . . . this phenomenal apparition" (*BA*, 397). But recognizing
the rarity of the image, she decides not to confide in the doctor. "I
knew," Sonie remarks, "that it was not a memory. But I concluded
that this morning was *not* the first time I had seen it, but that something in the external world upon which I could not lay my finger had
by accident dislodged it from the populous, diffuse, chimerical mazes
of my subconscious mind. I had this second time, as before, felt safe
and comforted. And it was because of this that I did not tell the doctor, out of the fear that if I told him, I would lose the room forever"
(*BA*, 398). The fear of the instability that such a vision may denote
leads Sonie to a new appreciation of Shura's condition and a more
temperate attitude toward the red room itself: "I had made a bargain
with my sense of duty: I said that the red room would be my refuge,
that when the time came I would resume the battle on the condition
that I might always return to it, as a warrior pauses to pray" (*BA*,
400).

Gradually, Sonie identifies the objects in the room. The book *Der
Traum den Rote Kammer* (*The Vision of the Red Room*) is in Miss
Pride's library; the writing desk is Louisa May Alcott's, which she
had seen on a tour of Concord. She recognizes the lobster-claw letter
opener that rests on the desk as belonging to an old woman in Chichester, and the wine as some that she had tasted one day at the
Countess von Happel's home. Now able to comprehend the elements
of the room, Sonie begins to feel comfortable with her microcosmic
refuge. She describes her vision as both "random daydream" and
"*deja vue*," a "sort of unlearned knowledge of the soul." The room
becomes for Sonie a sanctuary that assuages her pain: "Under my
own merciful auspices, I had made for myself a tamed-down sitting
room in a dead, a voiceless, city where no one could trespass, for I
was the founder, the governor, the only citizen" (*BA*, 414). Despite
her growing familiarity with its contents, however, Sonie remains
somewhat skeptical about the seductive attractions of the room. She

is afraid to retreat there too often and approaches the room only "when I felt that I could not withstand the onslaught of worry or of loneliness . . . then, I would turn to my ghost of a sanctuary as I might turn to a drug" (BA, 423).

When Sonie next withdraws to the red room, she has heard her mother's voice and sees, in the window across the courtyard, Miss Pride staring at her "with malevolent fixity." Sonie states, "I knew that my game had got out of control and that Miss Pride had found me out in my retreat and was judging me a lunatic" (BA, 465). She is "seized with a madness that was like an intense pain and was something outside myself, a violent force which urged my footsteps for the first time across the threshold onto the threadbare carpet with its faint green design. The knowledge that something external had precipitated my entrance was confused by a vertiginous and inarticulate emotion and for the present, I could not name the frenzy that had threatened but had not yet gained entrance" (BA, 465). So Sonie finally enters the room, to discover that a cushion makes the desk chair precisely the right height for her and that the feeling of serenity recurs. But her peace does not last. As Miss Pride's eyes pursue her, Sonie tries in vain to flee.

> I was strung out long like a bright wire that ended in brittle rays of copper, shining and pointed and raw. The eyes, like a surgeon's knives, were urged into my brain. The edges of the knives screamed like sirens; their sound curled in thin circles round my hot, pink brains. I crouched in a corner of the room, down behind the bookcase, safe, I thought. But I was plucked up by the burning yellow flares that went in a direct path like a sure blade. Miss Pride blinked her eyes. The room vanished. I had not moved but I felt an overwhelming tranquillity as if my brain were healed again, was sealed and rounded and impervious, was like a loaded, seamless ball, my hidden and wonderfully perfect pearl. (BA, 465–66)

Terrified by her close call with Miss Pride's piercing eyes, and therefore unable to appreciate the sense of "overwhelming tranquillity" that the experience leaves, Sonie is convinced that she must find the room before she goes mad. Seeking to understand the vision, she confides in Nathan, whose preoccupation with his own troubled life makes him oblivious of her confession. But Sonie really wants no audience, and the articulation of her secret helps her to comprehend its value.

> If Nathan had been listening to me as I told him what I had come for, if he had heard me taking off, layer by layer, the wrappings of my jewel, I

might have lost it forever. To my own ears, my revelation sounded banal, my terror was flaccid, unimportant, trumped-up. And I was surprised that I could not make him see what I so clearly saw myself: this churchly, peaceable hallucination. I had reached the end of my account and said, "I want to find the room, you see." But I was not really conscious of this need which, until now, had seemed so urgent, and when Nathan said, "I'm sorry, I haven't been listening. What did you say?" I was comforted that I had not, after all, admitted a trespasser. I returned to his immediate and frenzied world, feeling wise, mature, and safe. (*BA*, 473–74)

Sonie again seeks refuge in the room after her agreement to remain with Miss Pride indefinitely and her discovery that Shura will not recover, only to find that "the red room, now that I needed it, would not come" (*BA*, 484). Sonie does not yet know that she no longer needs the room, that the tranquillity and the healing are permanent and are the evidence of her victory over insanity. Her interior castle, the red room provides refuge and privacy as long as Sonie needs an escape from the exigencies of her life, but as she grows up, her increasing perceptiveness and maturity allow her to eschew the seductive and dangerous deep regions of the mind and to confront reality.

With Sonie's perspicuity comes a final full comprehension of Lucy Pride. It is in part Miss Pride's intrusion into the red room—and into Sonie's psyche—that forces Sonie to return from the unconscious, but her victory over insanity occurs more in spite of the predacious old woman than because of her. Sonie will stay on Pinckney Street; she is committed to her mentor, and she has nowhere else to go. Yet Sonie now accepts her relationship with her captor with a mature awareness of its possibilities and limitations. She knows that the lack of alternatives will tie her to Lucy Pride until the old woman's death, but she knows too that the woman is no mother, no acceptable role model.

Lucy Pride's limitations are legion, but her denial of her femininity, her inability to accept her sexuality, perhaps most disqualifies her as a paradigm for adult womanhood. In short, Miss Pride becomes increasingly exceptionable as Sonie not only learns more about her but outgrows childhood to assume a more complex existence. Another potential role model for Sonie, and a woman who is the antithesis of the masculine, ascetic Lucy Pride, is the Countess Berthe von Happel, a "large, fragrant Viennese" whose second marriage into an old Bostonian family has guaranteed her acceptance into the restrictive society that Sonie comes to inhabit. Voluptuous, exotic, verbose, and vain, the Countess shares nothing with Lucy Pride except an interest in stocks and bonds. She introduces Sonie into her private coterie of young admirers, and the girl becomes a regular at the woman's musical Fridays.

The vivacious Countess, so unlike the decorous Bostonians, is an attractive character, and Sonie, though she suspects that in many ways the affectionate woman is a fraud, becomes genuinely fond of her. She is nonetheless distressed by her friend's frequent caresses, which remind her of her mother's clinging embraces. When they meet, the Countess' "loving gesture," Sonie writes, "though it was only a part of her patronizing, impersonal manner, had made me think of my mother and had returned me directly, by no detours of specific memory, to the horror of womanly affection which I thought I had outgrown" (*BA*, 279).

The Countess calls Sonie and the other young women who frequent her music room "angel" and "darling." Although her caresses seem too obvious to be suspicious, the young men who adore her are known to betray "virile horror" at the sight of her kissing their female friends. The Countess' indifference to her male admirers is apparent, and Hopestill maintains that the Countess dislikes men: "She did not fear them, but she recoiled from them in a frigid, old-maidish way" (*BA*, 320). While the Countess prefers the company of women, Hopestill adds, she is not a lesbian, having "a stern, intuitive moral nature which kept her so under control that none but the most astute observer suspected anything irregular about her, but which allowed her to surround herself with girls, to caress them chastely, to send them presents, and to write them affectionate letters, indulgences permissible since they could have no consequences" (*BA*, 320).

Perhaps, as Hopestill claims, the Countess is not a lesbian, but Stafford seems to be offering yet another life-style for Sonie to observe. Annis Pratt notes that while early women authors could present sexual feelings between women because such desires were so taboo as to remain virtually unsuspected, after about 1920: "it became far less acceptable for woman authors to exhibit strong feelings between their heroes than during the previous era because an acknowledgment of lesbian sexuality had become more prevalent. It thus became more questionable to exhibit attractions between women than when the general public thought that women had no sexual urges and should be punished for taking a sexual initiative at all, even towards men."[7] Like Shura and Miss Pride, the Countess may well represent a sexual response and a mode of behavior that Sonie must reject.

In the heterogeneous personae of Shura, Lucy Pride, and the Countess, Stafford offers an intriguing variety of conduct and values that she gradually exposes as attractive but untenable. In Hopestill Mather, Miss Pride's niece and a fourth major female character in the novel, she presents Sonie with her most problematical, complex relationship. Throughout Sonie's early life in Chichester she is nearly as fascinated with the privileged girl as she is with her formidable aunt. Her first glimpse of Hopestill, at the Hotel, when she is ten and Sonie is nine, evokes Sonie's envy and establishes what is to become a lifelong relationship. As Sonie notes late in the novel, "There was a bond of sorts between us which, although she did not know it, went back to the day when I, a little girl, had first learned that she lived in this house" (*BA*, 346).

In *The Madwoman in the Attic*, Sandra Gilbert and Susan Gubar discuss the "mad double" in women's literature. Women are torn between their desire to please and defer, to act as an "angel," and their desire to exhibit the normal human anger and fears that earn them the label "monster," the authors claim. While most traditional female heroes are socially acceptable angels, "even the most apparently conservative and decorous women writers obsessively create fiercely independent characters who seek to destroy all the patriarchal structures which both their authors and their authors' submissive heroines seem to accept as inevitable." In *Madness and Sexual Politics in the Feminist Novel*, Barbara Hill Rigney offers a similar interpretation of the doppelgänger, or double, in women's fiction. She argues that while traditional interpretations of the doppelgänger view it as a manifestation of narcissism or as a defense against the destruction of the ego, in women's fiction "the doppelganger seems to represent the recognition of the tragedy of one's own fragmentation and alienation from the self." In much of women's writing, the protagonist, recognizing "that she has lost a self somewhere among the socially prescribed false selves which she has assumed, willingly or unwillingly, consciously or unconsciously," searches "for some rationale, some agent or helper to

7. *Ibid.*, 96.

heal the divided self—a mother. The protagonist inevitably finds, whether in an actual mother or in some other figure, a mirror image of her own split psyche, a doppelganger who is a manifestation of her schizophrenia."[8]

Throughout *Boston Adventure* Sonie is cognizant of being torn between two selves. Daydreaming at school, she says, "I would gradually float away, leaving my body behind, still sitting at the stained red desk," and become wealthy, blond Antoinette de la Mar (*BA*, 30). Later, when her teacher arranges for her to work for the family of her schoolmate Betty Brunson, Sonie finds that "one self" is convinced of the wisdom of the plan, while the other resists (*BA*, 69). Still later, her reaction to Miss Pride's suggestion that—because of her mother's insanity—she should not marry is to "lose her identity": "I was invaded by the strange feeling that I was not myself, or rather, that this was a phantom of myself, projected by my real being, still in Chichester" (*BA*, 314). All of her life Sonie is two people—one who lives in Chichester, another who resides in Boston. It is not difficult for her to honor Miss Pride's injunction to put aside her past when she begins her new life. Yet the old self remains. One February day, while she is riding with Hopestill, the unseasonable springlike weather evokes a sudden memory of "the day the year before when Miss Pride had come to take me in to Boston. There was little essential difference, I thought, between that version of myself who, shabby and with grimy fingernails had sat bewildered in the gloomy library and this one, pranked out in costly jodhpurs, waiting in a cramped and uncomfortable position for my skillful friend to ride back. There was a gross and disquieting discrepancy between my expensive clothes and my luxurious pastime and my little brother's unmarked grave" (*BA*, 326). Sonie's awareness of her divided self is an essential aspect of her search for an acceptable model of behavior, and having rejected her mother's stultifying psychosis and become increasingly disenchanted with Lucy Pride's devious rapacity, she turns, in the second half of the novel, as her search nears its end, to Hopestill.

Like Sonie, Hopestill is a misfit. Lazy, recalcitrant, a failure at school, she alienates Lucy Pride and her narrow Bostonian society by her association with bohemians in New York City and by her refusal

---

8. Gilbert and Gubar, *Madwoman in the Attic*, 77–78; Barbara Hill Rigney, *Madness and Sexual Politics in the Feminist Novel* (Madison, Wis., 1978), 10, 122.

to devote herself to the good works expected of Boston debutantes. She is acerbic, irreverent, and unpopular with her contemporaries in Boston. Despite Sonie's lifelong envy of the wellbred girl, the two become friends and allies. They share a relationship with Lucy Pride (interestingly, Hopestill's always strained relationship with her aunt deteriorates when Sonie enters their house) and an interest in Philip McAllister, widely perceived as the intended husband of Hopestill. Although Sonie is attracted to Philip from their first meeting, she is conscious of loving him only when Hopestill returns from New York, and her old envy is exacerbated by Philip's obvious desire for the pale, sensual redhead.

Time and proximity eventually overcome Sonie's resentment, and by the beginning of her second year in Boston she feels "free at last of any envy" of Miss Pride's niece (*BA*, 348). But the Hopestill who arrives from New York, after the summer, for her weekend visit in Boston, is a transformed woman. Gaunt and distraught, Hopestill confides to Sonie that she has been the patient, not—as her aunt and her friends believe—the student, of a fashionable psychoanalyst who treats "women who don't like their husbands for one reason or another or else don't have husbands and think they'll go off the deep end if they keep on living alone" (*BA*, 334). Suddenly stronger, and more mature and capable than Hopestill, Sonie feels a new empathy for the distressed girl. Originally angered by Hopestill's insistence one evening that she replace Sonie as Philip's date, she suddenly

> divined, through an intuition which had never been exercised in me before, either because of a physical immaturity or because of the want of circumstances, that there was a sole exigency that could drive her to this corner where, for all her insolence, she was terrified. And as I realized that not the satanic particles but the organic chemistry of her composition had led her to this replacement of myself for the evening (a replacement she was determined, I now knew, to make permanent), I was ready to withdraw any claims I might have had since her need was so much greater than my own. (*BA*, 357)

Sonie's silent recognition that Hopestill's hysteria and her renewed interest in Philip are the results of her pregnancy reinforces her identification with the girl. "Identifying my own body with Hopestill's to make my diagnosis of her altered nature," Sonie notes, "my comprehension had not been established by logic but by the completion of my own ripening" (*BA*, 358). Sonie's awareness of Hopestill's pregnancy, and thus her sexuality, stirs her own sexual desires, and "the elusive lover I had tried to construct was that unnamed, unacknowledged man whose impregnation of Hopestill was also an exegesis of my own changing self" (*BA*, 359). Sonie's peculiar friendship with Hopestill develops, as does her attraction to her friend's fiancé, and when the poised and confident Hopestill is displaced by a pregnant, desperate woman, Sonie recognizes their essential similarity. Now the relationship becomes symbiotic, an alliance of fellow sufferers, and Hopestill functions as a double, or doppelgänger, for the protagonist.

With the announcement of Hopestill and Philip's engagement, Sonie's jealousy is renewed. Both concerned about Hopestill's attempts to deceive her family and friends, and desolate at her own loss of Philip, she first escapes her misery (as well as her shame after a drunken interlude with Nathan that culminates in their dislocation of sleeping Lucy Pride) in the red room. As the wedding approaches, only Sonie, banished to her room for her "egregious misdemeanor," recognizes that Hopestill's despondency increases; only Sonie hears the girl's sobs as she escapes to her room (next door to Sonie's) for a respite from her prenuptial activities. And while Sonie yearns to comfort her friend, she hesitates to become involved in Hopestill's affairs because "beside a warm fire in a light room, an impression of the night's cold and darkness superimposes itself upon the altruistic impulse, and one rationalizes, says the cry comes from the throat of a drunk or of a cat that can sound like a woman or even that it is the lure of the thief" (*BA*, 419). Frustrated by her inability to assuage Hopestill's pain and the "vicarious fear" that her failure evokes, Sonie now willfully retreats to her imaginary sanctuary.

It is therefore Hopestill, perhaps even more than her aunt and Sonie's mother, who prompts Sonie's sojourn in the red room. The "wild, mad, and holy" doppelgänger, Rigney maintains, acts for the protagonist as "a guide in the exploration of the wild places of the self, the acceptance of which is always crucial." She continues, "Upon recognition of the doppelganger, each protagonist begins a descent into actual madness, or at least into the vicarious experience of madness as is the case with Jane Eyre and Clarissa Dalloway. Having descended, symbolically, into the flames where she consciously recognizes herself as 'insane' or potentially insane, each protagonist, phoenixlike, is able to surface as sane, equipped with an integrated self, an identity. It is this sense of identity which then permits her to cope effectively with what continues to be, nevertheless, an essentially hostile world."[9]

Sonie's forays into her unconscious do cause her to fear for her sanity, but in her lucid moments her response to Hopestill's predicament is self-authenticating: "While I did not minimize the discomfiture of my own position and spent a good part of every day in sorrowing over my unjust luck and even thought that in the end, my lot was much the worse, I felt that I was somehow better equipped to endure than Hopestill. She, the frail sheep lost from the herd, could not find her way back nor could she make her way alone" (*BA*, 419). The frail sheep marries, her pale face set in a death mask and her fingers, clutching her bouquet, "clenched like stone," and submits to a parodic marriage in which Philip, having discovered his wife's pregnancy, but unable to "burn a scarlet letter in her forehead," extracts his revenge by forcing upon Hopestill the constant presence and attentions of Harry Morgan, the unscrupulous father of her unborn child. Increasingly debilitated by Philip's subtle torture, Hopestill gradually deteriorates. "She seemed to have gone beyond fear and beyond rebellion, beyond, indeed, all feeling and to exist automatically. Perhaps she had surrendered completely to Philip's hatred and had allowed her physical being to share in her moral disintegration," Sonie observes (*BA*, 477). And her double's demoralization permits Sonie the recognition that frees her from the red room and madness, and allows her, strong and perceptive, to accept her integrated self. Continuing her ruminations about Hopestill's degeneration and the impairment of her beauty, Sonie wonders whether

what we had seen as beauty had not been beauty at all but another quality, an emotional or intellectual force so powerful that it actually appeared in her person. . . . Now it was not only Hopestill's illness that made me think she had always been ugly. There was a force at play in my altered perceptions that was subtler and stronger than that which had come from my expanding knowledge of beauty, or that gradual repudiation of childhood criteria, or that vision, enriched by maturity, which allows one to speak of "types of beauty." Rather, it was that I had slowly come of age in knowledge of her and of her *milieu* into which I had willed myself. What marked the advent of my adulthood was a mo-

9. Rigney, *Madness and Sexual Politics*, 122, 122–23.

ment when I . . . saw her lying bare-footed on the couch . . . I thought, "Why, it is her life that is ugly and has been from the beginning." (*BA*, 477–78)

Her epiphany and her journey to adulthood complete, Sonie can— and does—now abandon the red room. And with her recognition and acceptance of selfhood, she no longer needs Hopestill. "In order for . . . self-integration to occur," writes Rigney, "the doppelganger, who has represented the self as split, must in some way be annihilated or at least relegated to obscurity."[10] Hopestill, in a dramatic farewell to her fraudulent life, admits to Sonie that she has provoked her horse to throw her—has, in short, precipitated her own death. In the penultimate scene of the novel, Sonie visits her friend's grave in an attempt to "efface from my memory the unhappiness of her last days" and to understand her role in Hopestill's life; for, Sonie writes, "reason told me I was laughable and self-important in feeling myself an element in her death, but superstition rebuked me" (*BA*, 492). Departing from the cemetery, Sonie feels "strangely energetic and as if I had completed a difficult task" (*BA*, 494).

In *Boston Adventure*, Jean Stafford presents the maturation of a young woman and her growing recognition that the discovery and creation of a self necessitate a rejection of society's limitations. On her journey to adulthood, Sonie Marburg confronts seductive and frightening life-styles and temptations. Her exposure to and ultimate rejection of wealth, romance, madness, and emotional subjugation attest to her maturity and self-awareness. The conditions of her life necessitate compromise, but hers is a compromise chosen freely, with awareness and a realistic acceptance of her situation.

10. *Ibid.*, 123.

II
Growing Down
The Mountain Lion

Published in 1947, Jean Stafford's second novel, *The Mountain Lion*, rings intriguing variations on the themes and techniques of *Boston Adventure*. *The Mountain Lion* is shorter than its predecessor, and in it Stafford abandons the convoluted, discursive Jamesian sentences and philosophical musings of the first-person narration of the earlier novel for a third-person narration and a breezy, colloquial style. *The Mountain Lion* is lucid and controlled, at once linguistically economical and thematically complex. Critics have agreed that it is a more successful novel than *Boston Adventure*.[1]

Whereas in *Boston Adventure* Stafford juxtaposes the small fishing village of Chichester and Boston society, in *The Mountain Lion* her range broadens to include the vast American West. By associating life in Covina, the conventional town that is the setting of the first part of the novel, with the protagonists' mother's girlhood in St. Louis, Stafford expands the California setting to represent American middle-class, civilized (that is, eastern and feminine) life. Their iconoclastic grandfather convinces Molly and Ralph, the young protago-

---

1. See Auchincloss, *Pioneers and Caretakers*, 93; Ihab Hassan, "Jean Stafford: The Expense of Style and the Scope of Sensibility," *Western Review*, XIX (Spring, 1955), 191; Review of Jean Stafford's *The Mountain Lion*, *New Yorker*, March 8, 1947, pp. 97–98.

nists, that "California was not the West but was a separate thing like Florida and Washington, D.C.," and Stafford corroborates this assertion by contrasting the Covina life-style with that on Grandpa's Colorado ranch, which is universalized to represent the West by its similarity to his other spreads in Missouri, Texas, and Oklahoma (*ML*, 8). The East vs. West dichotomy, a major theme of *The Mountain Lion* as well as of many of Stafford's short stories, allows Stafford to explore a series of polarities that includes innocence and experience, youth and adulthood, and nature and civilization. These polarities both manifest and develop her complex ironic vision.

The Mountain Lion is the story of Molly and Ralph Fawcett, who, aged eight and ten respectively as the novel begins, are pale, gawky children with "bad uneven teeth and nearsighted eyes so that they had to wear braces and spectacles. Their skin and hair and eyes were dark and the truth of it was that they always looked a little dirty" (*ML*, 28). Ugly and sickly, the siblings have nothing in common with their attractive, poised, older twin sisters; and, both precocious and cowardly, they have no friends: "Ralph and Molly had none but one another" (*ML*, 29). United against the world, Ralph and Molly, as the novel opens, anxiously await the annual autumnal visit of Grandpa Kenyon, a rumpled, coarse old man who, like his grandchildren, is uncomfortable in civilized society. Soon after his arrival, Grandpa Kenyon dies suddenly, and the following summer Molly and Ralph visit his son Claude on his Colorado ranch. The siblings escape their stifling life in California during three summer visits—and a final, dramatic year—with Uncle Claude.

In *Boston Adventure* Jean Stafford created, in Sonie Marburg, the first of her many child and adolescent protagonists who are grappling with the vicissitudes of their young lives. Alienated from her family during her childhood and from xenophobic Boston in her adolescence, Sonie struggles to comprehend her world and to find her place in it. Her alternatives are a stultifying but comfortable life as Lucy Pride's companion, and a retreat into the interior castle, the safe but illusory caverns of her own mind. Sonie overcomes the temptations of the red room, her personal interior castle, and ultimately embraces adult realities by compromising on an existence with Miss Pride. Paradoxically, in the shorter work *The Mountain Lion* Stafford distends her treatment of the initiation theme to present not only the attractions and difficulties but the repercussions of both options. Ralph illustrates the urge toward acculturation and inevitable compromise that Sonie ultimately fulfills, while Molly, somewhat inexplicably denied the solace of the interior castle, plays out the retreat from the world that Sonie's red room allows. With Ralph and Molly, Stafford presents both acceptance and rejection of the demands of growing up, and creates, in effect, a double *Bildungsroman*.[2] In her investigation of male and female responses to the experience of growing up, Stafford continues her examination of the female's search for authenticity and selfhood in an inimical world.

As *The Mountain Lion* begins, Molly and Ralph are virtual twins. Having been stricken simultaneously the year before with scarlet fever, they are left with a glandular disorder that manifests itself in nosebleeds, which nearly always occur at the same time (*ML*, 3). Their ailment sends them home from school early on the day that Grandpa Kenyon is to arrive, and on the walk home they affirm their camaraderie and innocence in an unconscious baptismal rite. In the small ditches that line the road, "Now and again they stopped and dipped their handkerchiefs and wiped the blood off their hands and arms" (*ML*, 4). The siblings' similarities and their existence in a private world of jokes and rituals reinforce their alienation from the world around them and inspire a wary caution in their family and friends: "There were times when Mrs. Fawcett feared for the reason of her two younger children: they had natures of such cold determination that she trembled to think what they might do if they were crossed in a matter very close to their hearts" (*ML*, 15).

Ralph and Molly's symbiotic relationship and their partnership in their alienation from their surroundings make their awkward lives tolerable. They do not fit in the effete, conventional society of Covina that is exemplified by their oppressive mother. She, denuded of her cultured St. Louis girlhood when her father, Grandfather Bonney, died and her mother married an uncultured rancher named Kenyon, strives to recreate for her fatherless children the decorous life-style that her own father, a fastidious button manufacturer, represents. Because her father's death resulted from blood poisoning contracted from a scratch from a paddock nail, Mrs. Fawcett forbids her children

2. See Charlotte Goodman's examination of *The Mountain Lion*, as well as *Wuthering Heights, The Mill on the Floss, My Antonia*, and *them*, in "The Lost Brother, the Twin: Women Novelists and the Male-Female Double *Bildungsroman*," *Novel*, XVII (Fall, 1983), 28–43.

to experience "everything . . . that was attended by the least possibility of danger" (*ML*, 14). They cannot climb trees, or own bicycles or roller skates; and their pastimes consist of board games, the painting of watercolors, and poetry recitations conducted in a house that is cluttered with a "flurry of little objects, little vases and boxes on gilt tables and whatnots hanging in the corners" (*ML*, 97). Stafford views this prissy, sterile environment with the same sardonic eye that she casts on Boston society in *Boston Adventure*. The Fawcetts' neighbors, Reverend Follansbee, a voluble bore with a pinched face and a digestive condition, and his catarrhal wife, are country cousins to the more cultured snobs on Pinckney Street. On their frequent visits they pay ludicrous homage to the memory of Grandfather Bonney, a plump, bald, well-dressed gentleman whose greatest achievement is that he once met Grover Cleveland. Grandfather Bonney presides over the house, his portrait gracing the parlor and his ashes resting in an urn on the mantel, and for Ralph and Molly, as for Stafford, he symbolizes the smug, respectable life of the Fawcett family, a life that the young deviants can sustain only because they have each other.

Although Molly's childhood is not as onerous as Sonie's, the homely, sensitive child is no less estranged from her existence. While Sonie escapes her disquiet in the chimera of a life in Boston with Lucy Pride, Molly seeks comfort in her relationship with her brother. Molly idolizes Ralph; older, wiser, and male, he verifies her worth with his love. She follows and emulates the boy whose embrace comforts her, whose rejection destroys her. But early in the novel, a more mature Ralph begins to recognize that their alliance is more willed than innate. He resents Molly's adoration, her repetition of his jokes and her narration of his dreams.

> There was only one thing about Molly he did not like, Ralph decided, and that was the way she copied him. It was natural for her to want to be a boy (who *wouldn't!*) but he knew for a fact she couldn't be. Last week, he had had to speak sharply to her about wearing one of his outgrown Boy Scout shirts: he was glad enough for her to have it, but she had not taken the "Be Prepared" thing off the pocket and he had to come out and say brutally, "Having that on a girl is like dragging the American flag in the dirt." (*ML*, 29–30)

When Grandpa Kenyon arrives, joining Ralph in the fussy feminine environment, the boy reaffirms his resentment of Molly and his de-

sire for male companionship. But Grandpa's death reunites the siblings, who share their fear and grief in a silent embrace: "'I'm scared,'
[Molly] said, taking his hand. 'I don't want him to be dead, Ralph. I
don't *want* him to be!' They lay down on the floor beside the coffin,
sobbing in each other's arms, but making scarcely any noise lest the
ladies and their sisters hear them" (*ML*, 54). The reconciliation, however, is short-lived, for to Ralph's delight, Uncle Claude, who arrives
for his father's funeral, is "a younger and slighter version of Grandpa"
(*ML*, 59). Recognizing that Claude is as uncomfortable with Mrs.
Fawcett and the Follansbees as his father was, Ralph's aversion to his
conventional family intensifies. Although his shyness prevents him at
first from befriending his uncle, "He was determined not to let him go
. . . without explaining to him that he and Molly were different from
the rest of the family" (*ML*, 66). But Molly, it seems, is too different.
After reading one of his sister's curious poems, Ralph decides that
Molly is going crazy, and his fear of losing his only ally prompts him to
seek out Claude, whose quiet strength and interest in Ralph convince
the boy that he has found a new friend.

The next summer, their first trip to the strange, forbidding ranch
reconciles Ralph and Molly for a time, though Ralph notices that his
pitiful sister looks more incongruous than ever in her frilly dress. He
decides that Molly is not going crazy, that she's simply different from
other people, and perceives that although "he liked her when they
were alone . . . she embarrassed him in public because she said such
peculiar things" (*ML*, 94).

As his initial fear of the primitive, mountainous landscape and the
rugged ranch hands abates, Ralph becomes increasingly fascinated
with Claude and the rough male world of the ranch. He learns to ride
and begins to help Claude with the chores, leaving Molly more and
more often on her own. And Molly, an alien in the refined world of her
mother and sisters, is all the more estranged in this man's world.
Claude, though he likes the lonely young boy, is perplexed by acerbic
Molly and strives—albeit unconsciously—to separate her from her
brother. Although when they are riding, Ralph notes, "Uncle Claude
occasionally praised him and his confidence grew . . . he was so mean
to Molly ('You set on that bench like a sack of potatoes,' he would say
to her) that she seldom went with them but stayed home to help in the
garden or to write" (*ML*, 104–105).

Their return to California marks another renewal of Molly and Ralph's friendship, but their relationship is close only in the inimical environment of Covina. At the ranch in the summer, Ralph, with his increasing aptitude for riding and shooting, no longer needs Molly. He recalls a day late in their first summer in Colorado when Molly "looked up at him, her large humble eyes fondling his face with lonely love, [and] he wanted to cry out with despair because hers was really the only love he had and he found it nothing but a burden and a tribulation" (*ML*, 116).

Molly is increasingly an encumbrance to Ralph because, while he matures and grows in his awareness of life, she stubbornly refuses to change. Filled with wonder at the sight of the birth of a calf, Ralph tries to share his awe with Molly, but "when he told [her] about it, she stuck her fingers in her ears and screamed at him . . . 'You're a dirty liar!' and her nose began to bleed" (*ML*, 118). And when Mrs. Fawcett announces that the family will move to the East when Ralph, in fulfillment of Grandfather Bonney's wishes, enrolls at Harvard, Molly insists that she and Ralph will marry each other and remain in Covina with Grandpa Kenyon (*ML*, 124–25). At twelve, Molly's rejection of acceptable sexuality is as naïve and recalcitrant as her insistence, four years earlier, that she did not want Grandpa Kenyon to be dead. Ralph, on the other hand, is obsessed with his dawning awareness of sexuality. Although he is confused by his strange yearnings and by the physical changes that accompany them, he recognizes that it is natural for him to grow strong and healthy, and wonders why Molly remains ugly and lanky: "There was something wrong with her and while he still loved her, he wished oftener and oftener that she did not exist" (*ML*, 128).

When Mrs. Fawcett decides to take her beloved twins on a journey around the world, she proposes that Molly and Ralph spend the year on the ranch with Claude, claiming that they are happier in Colorado than at home (to which Molly responds, with typical acerbity, "I do not believe in happiness" [*ML*, 136]). On the train ride, Ralph, frightened by his increasing preoccupation with sexuality and his recent fantasies about his older sisters, clings again to Molly: "He thought of her as if she were the last foothold beneath which the world fell away in a chasm: it would be so easy to lose his footing, relax his finger-holds, and plunge downward to wedge his bones in a socket of rocks.

Vile fogs baffled him and vileness was below him. Molly, alone, he thought, did not urge him to corruption" (*ML*, 158). As the train enters a tunnel, which Ralph, with unconscious recognition of its Freudian symbolism, interprets as "an apotheosis of his own black, sinful mind," he loses his precarious foothold and whispers to his sister, "Molly, tell me all the dirty words you know." The moment is climactic: "Ralph's childhood and his sister's expired at that moment of the train's entrance into the surcharged valley. It was a paradox, for now they should be going into a tunnel with no end, now that they had heard the devil speak" (*ML*, 158–59).

Ralph's overt violation of the silent taboo against sexuality changes forever his relationship with his sister. Having articulated his sexual desires, he abandons the innocent world that Molly tenaciously (but, as she ages, increasingly tentatively) clings to, and leaves his awkward sibling alone in her prelapsarian universe. The epiphanic moment notwithstanding, the train ride marks the end of Ralph's guardianship of Molly because it brings their permanent residence in a distinctly male environment. Now that he has successfully renounced the feminine world of his mother and twin sisters, a physically mature Ralph can accomplish his emotional maturity in a man's world. But his adulthood is contingent upon his rejection of the lingering vestiges of childhood; he can embrace his manhood only as he discards his youth. And the symbol of Ralph's childhood is his sister Molly.

Like Sonie, Ralph achieves his adulthood in part through his interaction with adults who are for him models of mature behavior. Denied a father and having rejected the narrow-minded, cruel Mr. Follansbee, he has originally only his taciturn, peripatetic grandfather to look to for guidance and verification. The old man's inability to conform to social expectations reinforces his grandson's dissatisfaction with his life among women. When Ralph discovers in his Uncle Claude a more accessible father figure and withdraws to Claude's intrinsically male environment, he takes a major step toward accomplishing his own maturity. Much of the novel, which is presented primarily from Ralph's point of view, chronicles the boy's increasing understanding of the value and limitations of his uncle's concept of masculinity, his gradual recognition that Claude's inability to react emotionally to life and death are the results of his failure to grow up. Ralph's relationship with Claude, whose sexuality, leadership, and diligence offer the boy a pattern of male conduct that he can initially emulate and eventually transcend, leads him through a difficult adolescence to the edge of an acceptable adulthood.

Poor Molly, on the other hand, whose unattractiveness and intelligence disqualify her from participation in the stereotypically feminine world of her mother and sisters, has no acceptable female role model. Unlike Sonie, Molly is denied even a conditional mother figure and is therefore jettisoned in a male world without love or guidance. Her mother is too preoccupied with her nostalgic memories of her lost girlhood in St. Louis and her pride in her refined twin daughters to concern herself with her younger children. Her interactions with Molly and Ralph are limited to warnings "about their clean clothes or getting too much sunlight" and oppressive supervision of their indoor activities. When they use watercolors, for example, "Mrs. Fawcett guided their fingers so expertly and so patiently that the results made everyone believe the children were unusually gifted" (*ML*, 14, 78). Despite his mother's obsessive fears about the dangers of life on the ranch, Ralph recognizes that she "was secretly glad to be rid of her volatile two in the summer and to bask in the sunny dispositions and pretty faces of her two older children" (*ML*, 121).

While both Ralph and Molly perplex their conventional mother, it is Molly who most unnerves the proper Mrs. Fawcett. Although she is suspicious of Claude's influence on Ralph, she welcomes the improvements that summers at the ranch bring to her son. Molly, unfortunately, seems a hopeless case: "The depths of this child were unfathomable and Mrs. Fawcett at times was really afraid of her. Somehow time did not soften her, did not make her have thoughts and feelings like other children" (*ML*, 123). Mrs. Fawcett is afraid of Molly because she defies all definitions of femininity. She is too homely, too meanspirited, and too smart: "Everyone said that she had the brains in the family, but as Mrs. Fawcett was not interested in brains, she thought this a handicap rather than otherwise and often told Molly that there were other things in life besides books" (*ML*, 143–144). The other things, her mother would have Molly believe, are Scotch-plaid gingham dresses, Cashmere Bouquet, and polite visits to the Follansbees—which her delicate sisters, with their soft golden hair and "the poise of ladies of thirty," enjoy. Tall, round-shouldered Molly, with her coarse, straight black hair and swarthy complexion, is

both unwilling and unable to emulate her superficial, empty-headed
sisters. For her, one of the attractions of the ranch is that it provides
a respite from the onerous presence of Leah and Rachel.

At the ranch, Claude and his cowboys, though they proudly exist in
a man's world of "catalogues from L. L. Bean and Montgomery Ward,
boxes of buckshot, fly-books, [and] odd bits of leather and metal," suffer the presence of the women who serve them (*ML*, 97). The house-
keeper, Mrs. Brotherman, welcomes Molly's interest and help in the
garden ("Poor Molly, so unflowerlike," her brother notes, "should
have been interested in something like minerals, but she loved flowers" [*ML*, 168–169]), but, "a fragile, dispirited gentlewoman who
appeared to find everything in the world immeasurably sad," she has
neither the strength to manage nor the spirit to appeal to the likes of
Molly (*ML*, 90). Her daughter Winifred, who serves the food, cleans,
and makes the beds at the ranch, is a lively teenager whose profi-
ciency with a rifle and on horseback intimidates Ralph and Molly. She
befriends the young greenhorns, however, and wins their affection by
teaching them to survive in the rugged environment. Ralph and
Molly both develop crushes on the lean tomboy, but Winifred too
grows up. By their fourth summer in Colorado, she is "plump . . . and
so mature and feminine that Ralph could not recognize in her the
shooting companion of earlier summers, that rather negative and taciturn person who, without playing a role, had seemed like another boy.
Now she was a positive creature, self-assured, beautiful and glowing
with an interior smile" (*ML*, 172). The smiling Winifred is in love and
engaged, and a decidedly unplump, unfeminine Molly condemns
Winifred's betrayal by dramatically and irrevocably adding her name
to the list of unforgivables, her sacred registry of everyone she has
ever known (including, eventually, Ralph) except her father and
Grandpa Kenyon.

Molly finds one soul mate in Magdalene, the ancient black cook
whose misanthropy is so virulent that it terrifies even Molly. Shriv-
eled and ugly, the "bluish gray" old woman "was always smoldering
with an inward rage or a vile amusement over something sexual or
something unfortunate, and she spoke chiefly in obscene or blas-
phemous expletives" (*ML*, 98). Outcast meets outcast; Molly and
Magdalene understand each other: "You're a nigger," Molly angrily
accuses the old woman, and she replies, "You're pore white trash"

(*ML*, 176). Such is Molly's self-image that, in an unconscious rejection of her mother and acceptance of her incapacity to function in her world, she decides that she is the daughter of the repugnant, rancorous old woman, who recognizes no such kinship with the girl.

Molly, in short, once Ralph alienates her, has no one. Her quest for selfhood is thwarted by her existence in a male environment and her failure to discover a female guide for her journey. Shunned by her family, labeled as unsightly and obstreperous, she embodies the feminine fictional paradigm that Annis Pratt labels "the Growing-Up-Grotesque Archetype." In the contemporary woman's *Bildungsroman*, as in early novels of female development, Pratt maintains, "the young hero sets forth with wit and intelligence only to be punished by an internalized form of self-torture with which she programs herself into atrophy and disuse."[3]

While Ralph's exposure to the arduous reality of the ranch improves his health and his appearance, Molly seems determined to aggravate their estrangement and her misery by increasingly self-destructive behavior. When Ralph explains that they cannot marry each other, her punishment for her brother is to pour acid over her hand. As the skin blisters and the stench rises from her burning skin, she begins to cry, "not with pain but with terror at this odor of her destruction" (*ML*, 130). When the doctor tells Mrs. Fawcett that she must watch the girl's wound for signs of infection, "Molly's heart said, 'Goody! Goody!'" and she is pleased to learn that the burn will leave an unsightly scar (*ML*, 134). After the elaborate ritual of her bath, Molly punishes her abhorrent body by tightly binding her stomach with flannel, and goes to bed with wet hair in the hope of contracting tuberculosis. Molly's feelings of inadequacy, her inability to find or accept her self, are symbolized by her repudiation of her body. "I know I'm ugly. I know everybody hates me. I wish I were dead," she jealously screams at Ralph when she catches him talking to a female schoolmate (*ML*, 139). "She took a vindictive pleasure in her plainness. She would stand before the mirror in the hall and when someone passed by would point to her reflection and say, 'Admit I'm prettier than Mary Pickford'" (*ML*, 144).

Molly's perverse delight in her unattractiveness is complicated by

3. Pratt, *Archetypal Patterns in Women's Fiction*, 31.

her passionate resistance to any awareness of sexuality. Her horror at Ralph's "outrage" on the train provokes her to add his name to her list of unforgivables. She contemplates Ralph's abominable behavior in her bath (which is a complicated procedure partly because Molly— as Freud would be interested to note—never sits in the tub while the water is running for fear that a snake might come through the faucet), undistracted by her body because she thinks of herself "as a long wooden box with a mind inside" (*ML*, 177). Ralph's request, she decides, is another example of "all that tommyrot with which people were constantly trying to ruin her life" (*ML*, 182).

Alienated not only from the ranch and its inhabitants—including her brother—but from herself as well, Molly enacts another of the traditional motifs of the female novel of development. In the "Green-World Archetype," the adolescent girl discovers an oasis in an extra-human environment. In nature, the young protagonist finds "solace, companionship, and independence. . . . Nature . . . becomes an ally of the woman hero, keeping her in touch with her selfhood, a kind of talisman that enables her to make her way through the alienations of male society."[4] Toward the end of the novel, as Ralph becomes increasingly obsessed with Goldilocks, the elusive mountain lion that he and Claude want to shoot, Molly seeks solace and solitude in the mountains. At Garland Peak she discovers a small, secluded glade, the perfect "study" where she can write without disruption. The glade is her private place, the symbol of her isolation and of her inviolate self: "It seemed to Molly when she was alone in the mountains that she had been by herself for years now, really ever since Grandpa had died. It was as if Ralph and her mother and sisters were no blood kin to her at all, as if nobody ever had been except her father and Grandpa Kenyon, who was really only what you called 'a connection'" (*ML*, 209).

Just before Christmas, Ralph and Claude accompany Molly to Garland Peak to cut a fir tree, and while there they catch a glimpse of Goldilocks. Molly has never seen an animal during her solitary visits to the peak, and awed by the power and beauty of the mountain lion and annoyed by the male intrusion into her sanctuary, she is "afraid and thought she could never come here again" (*ML*, 211). Thinking

4. *Ibid.*, 21.

later of the graceful cat, Molly becomes sad and is "full of wishes. She wished that she had yellow hair like Leah's and Rachel's and the lion's. She wished she could go to London and become a famous writer. She wished she did not have to wear glasses; she wished she were only four feet five" (*ML*, 212). When Mrs. Brotherman expresses her fear of Goldilocks, Molly feels that she will not be safe in the mountains until the animal is dead. Alone in her room, Molly "could not keep her mind on anything; it kept darting around like a darning needle and she did not know what was the matter with her. If she only had yellow hair, she thought, she would be an entirely different kind of person; she would not be cross all the time" (*ML*, 214). Increasingly irritable, Molly denounces Ralph and Uncle Claude for violating her retreat ("They had *known* that she never saw any wild animals when she was alone and they had come today deliberately so that everything would be ruined" [*ML*, 214]), condemns Christmas as "bourgeois," and appends Winifred's name to her list. Finally, in her ultimate act of self-immolation, "She reached for her diary and her pencil and to the list of unforgivables she added her own name. She burst into tears and cried until she was hungry, and all the time she watched herself in the mirror, getting uglier and uglier until she looked like an Airedale" (*ML*, 217).

Molly does not understand that the intrusion of men into her private sanctum is the ultimate violation of the self, what Pratt calls the "Rape Trauma Archetype." Pratt remarks, "Social expectations for a young woman's destiny surface in women's fiction as a division of loyalties between the hero's green-world authenticity and the social world of enclosure . . . we see men pictured as agents of harsh disruption."[5] Ralph and Claude's penetration into Molly's glade dispossesses her of her only sanctuary from the outside world, making her life ineffectual. After she has dramatically placed herself in the execrable company of the unforgivables, she says little, and the story is henceforth almost exclusively Ralph's tale.

In the spring, on the day after Molly's graduation from eighth grade, she, Ralph, and Winifred drive to Garland Peak for a picnic, where they are to be joined later by Claude. Ralph, increasingly entranced with Goldilocks and worried that his mother's imminent re-

5. *Ibid.*, 25.

turn from Europe will take him away from the ranch before he is able to capture his prey, is distracted and annoyed by Molly. He knows that she has not forgiven him for his reprehensible conduct on the train, and he suspects that she will "save up" her knowledge of his corruption and "use it when the right time came" (*ML*, 226). Sadly, Ralph recalls the night when he and Molly shared their silent grief on the floor beside Grandpa's coffin and notes that "nothing had ever been really right since then, but why? . . . 'I'll never be happy again,' he said softly and aloud. Neither would Molly, but Molly did not want to be happy and she wanted him to be as wretched as she" (*ML*, 227). Vaguely, Ralph blames Molly for their unhappiness; for him, her willful refusal to surrender her innocence is a lingering repudiation of his festering adolescence. And when Molly threatens to tell Winifred what Ralph uttered in the tunnel, he warns her, "Molly, if you tell, I'll . . ." (*ML*, 225).

Upset with Molly, Ralph takes off alone and, sighting Goldilocks in a glade near a flat rock, violates his agreement not to hunt the animal without Claude and shoots. A second shot announces his uncle's presence, and when, finding the bullet hole, Ralph sees that it is not his shot that has killed the cat, he is "sick with failure." Seconds later, a sound in the nearby bushes, "a bubbling of blood . . . from a human throat," distracts the men.

> Molly lay beside a rotten log, a wound like a burst fruit in her forehead. Her glasses lay in fragments on her cheeks and the frame, torn from one ear, stuck up at a raffish angle. The elastic had come out of one leg of her gym bloomers and it hung down to her shin. The sound in her throat stopped. Uncle Claude knelt down beside her, but Ralph stood some paces away. He could as clearly see the life leave her as you could see fire leave burnt-out wood. It receded like a tide, lifted like a fog. . . . "I didn't see her! . . . I didn't hear her! I didn't kill her!" (*ML*, 229)

Ralph *has* killed Molly—accidentally, tragically, yet inevitably. Reviewers contemporary with Stafford and later critics have remarked about the sudden violence of the novel's denouement. Blanche H. Gelfant, in her discussion of the "subversion of form and myths and manners" in *The Mountain Lion*, maintains that Molly's "death effects the most complete revolution, turning the book we have been enjoying as comedy to pathos and melodrama." Like the mountain lion, Molly is a symbol of a "virginal, childhood, uncontaminated *something* that is inevitably lost in growing up," and therefore, like the animal, must die, writes Louis Auchincloss. Stuart L. Burns, in "Counterpoint in Jean Stafford's *The Mountain Lion*," concurs: "A shared quality of isolation links Molly most closely and directly with Goldilocks . . . both are the prey of a hostile society." William T. Pilkington also claims that they must both die "because both are misfits who somehow threaten to disrupt the delicately balanced social arrangements that encircle them."[6]

The mountain lion, which enters the novel only after the climactic scene in the tunnel, symbolizes Molly's vulnerable selfhood. A female, the cat is endowed with human characteristics; Claude names her Goldilocks because she is "as blonde as a movie star." Affirming her alliance with the animal, Molly wishes for yellow hair like the cat's (*ML*, 170). After Ralph and Claude shoot, Ralph caresses the fallen animal and, portending his imminent discovery of his slain sister, whispers: "She's so little . . . she isn't any bigger than a dog. She isn't as *big*." Moments later, he strokes his sister's bloodstained face. "Molly," he says. "Molly girl" (*ML*, 228, 230).

Obstinately unattractive and perversely misanthropic, Molly does not—and is determined that she will not—accept the realities of adulthood. Like the mountain lion, which is among the last of a vanishing species in the now civilized American West, she is an anomaly. The adolescent who will not abandon the illusions and naïveté of childhood cannot survive in a viable culture and must be eliminated. So, as the masculine Miss Pride intrudes upon Sonie's red room and forces her to confront reality, Ralph, who is, in hunting Goldilocks, enacting the male ritual of initiation, invades Molly's solitary retreat and invalidates her isolation. It is therefore not merely her innocence that destroys Molly but her "otherness." She is a misfit in Covina, but she creates a life there, however estranged. At the ranch, the most patriarchal of societies, Molly is a double threat, risking by her very existence not only her own maturity but her brother's as well. If Ralph is to grow up, Molly has to go.

6. Blanche H. Gelfant, "Revolutionary Turnings: *The Mountain Lion* Reread," *Massachusetts Review*, XX (Spring, 1979), 117; Auchincloss, *Pioneers and Caretakers*, 155; Stuart L. Burns, "Counterpoint in Jean Stafford's *The Mountain Lion*," *Critique*, IX (Spring, 1967), 27; William T. Pilkington, Introduction to Jean Stafford's *The Mountain Lion* (Albuquerque, 1972), xiv–xv.

Chester E. Eisinger, in *Fiction of the Forties*, recognizes that Molly's existence threatens her brother's selfhood: "She comes to represent for him, all unknowingly, the feminine principle that stands as the obstacle to the full expression of his maleness. In the inevitable assertion of his manhood as part of the individuation process, he kills his sister . . . in an accident that is the unconscious expression of his wish." Gelfant concurs.

> When early in the novel Ralph cries, "Golly *Moses*, I'd like to go out West," he expresses the pristine wish of the mythic figure of the American culture—the roving young hero who leaves civilization for the still uncontaminated places in the continent . . . where he can enact the timeless ritual of initiation to manhood. . . . For the West is the symbolic country where boys become men; and where girls, even the closest of sisters, become not only extraneous or intrusive, but also threatening. As a female, Molly encumbers Ralph in his obsessive stalking of the mountain lion and the masculinity that is his trophy. Her constant presence reminds him of a part of himself he can no longer endure, and indeed must annihilate, if he is to grow up—the feminine part of his nature.[7]

In *The Mountain Lion* Jean Stafford expands the examination of the female adolescent experience that she undertook first in *Boston Adventure*. Raised in a patriarchal society, albeit one that betrays the advantages and limitations of a feminine, civilizing influence, Sonie Marburg constructs from the alternative feminine life-styles that surround her one that offers the possibilities for survival in a man's world. Lucy Pride's example is restrictive and oppressive, and realistic Stafford allows no real hope that Sonie will escape the sacrificial victimization that her fate at the end of the novel promises. Yet, however tragically, Sonie does survive. Sad little Molly, bereft in an unadulterated masculine environment and denied the guidance and example of acceptable female models, cannot survive. In the author's note to the 1972 reprint of *The Mountain Lion*, Jean Stafford, recognizing the tragic inevitability of Molly's fate, expresses her "remorse" for "what I had done to my heroine, Molly Fawcett. . . . Poor old Molly! I loved her dearly and I hope she rests in peace" (*ML*, xvii, xix). In her affection for Molly, Stafford loved and mourned—as readers of the

7. Chester E. Eisinger, *Fiction of the Forties* (Chicago, 1963), 299; Gelfant, "Revolutionary Turnings," 120–21.

novel do—that innocence that adulthood purloins and that Ralph must now live without. Stafford's affection and regret are understandable, for in the fictional world of *The Mountain Lion*, there is nothing else that she could have done to Molly and nothing that she could have done for her.

III
Living upon Wreckage
The Catherine Wheel

In 1952, with the publication of *The Catherine Wheel*, Jean Stafford the author grew up. Her third and final novel is her finest, affirming, with its depth of vision and control of technique, an artistic maturity that *Boston Adventure* and *The Mountain Lion* lack. Ihab Hassan welcomed in *The Catherine Wheel* the development from satire to irony and sensibility, and praised the novel's "warmth and bounty of apprehension, a certain resonance which is like the resonance of a legend." Chester E. Eisinger pronounced the novel "the finest example of its kind that the new fiction produced in the years after the war. . . . *The Catherine Wheel* is a disciplined and completed book."[1]

The Catherine Wheel is the story of one summer in the lives of Katharine Congreve and her young cousin Andrew Shipley. As the novel begins Andrew and his older twin sisters have just arrived in Hawthorne, Maine, for their annual summer visit with Cousin Katharine at idyllic Congreve House. Desolated by the discovery that his one friend, Victor Smithwick, is preoccupied with nursing his older brother who has recently returned from sea with a mysterious illness, Andrew is further distressed by the perception that Katharine,

1. Hassan, "Jean Stafford: The Expense of Style and the Scope of Sensibility," 194; Eisinger, *Fiction of the Forties*, 302.

his sensitive, sympathetic "second mother," is distractedly unaware of his disappointment.

Katharine's attention this summer is directed inward and backward. Perplexed by the assault of sudden trances, momentary journeys of fear that attenuate her consciousness, Katharine reflects on her life—her love at seventeen for young John Shipley and her loss of him to her cousin Maeve; her lifelong grief concealed by the veneer of an enviable friendship with John, Maeve, and their children, Andrew and the twins; and now, twenty years later, her bitter triumph when John returns to her and begs her to run off with him. Recognizing her repressed resentment of Maeve and obsessed with her guilt over having agreed to flee with John if, after another summer abroad with Maeve, he cannot continue with his marriage, Katharine comes to fear Andrew, who reminds her of his father and whose sullen behavior, she believes, reflects his knowledge of her secret guilt. But Andrew knows nothing of his father's relationship with Katharine and is himself preoccupied with his increasing abhorrence of the sailor who has usurped his only friend. Ironically, he becomes certain that Katharine has intuited his own guilty desire for Charles Smithwick's death. Their mutual distrust and inability to communicate exacerbate their personal torment and end only with Katharine's violent, fiery immolation on the final night of summer.

The Catherine Wheel shares many of the characteristics of Stafford's other fiction. Andrew, like Sonie Marburg, Ralph and Molly Fawcett, and innumerable protagonists of the short stories, is an alienated adolescent. Small and shy, he is poor at sports and unpopular at school. Excluded from the "inner oneness" of his twin sisters, he has nothing in common with his sickly, vapid mother and despises his feckless, irascible father (*CW*, 55). This opposition of the worlds of children and adults is a typical Stafford theme. Andrew's now-elusive childhood pastimes of clamming, exploring, and harassing the town's inhabitants with Victor are contrasted with the peaceful, enervated ritual of tea and quiet conversation that Katharine and the elderly residents of Hawthorne share. Antithetical too are this tranquil summer existence and the bustling, workday world of Boston. Andrew cherishes his aestival respites from the demands of the winter urban world, and Katharine, who spends half the year in Boston, is "not really contented anywhere except in Congreve House"

(*CW*, 62). Her sophisticated friends complain about the monotony of life in Hawthorne, and Katharine, articulating Stafford's interest in the lives of the very young and the very old, admits that it "had nothing at all to offer any generation except the oldest and the newest, no club, no proper swimming beach, no summer theater, no sailboat races" (*CW*, 64). Katharine loves Hawthorne and its ancient inhabitants for their apparent immunity to change. Like Lucy Pride, she preserves the past with her refusal to abandon her "anachronistic black brougham," her old-fashioned garb, and her formal dinner parties (*CW*, 30). This contrast of past and present is one of the central themes of *The Catherine Wheel*. Throughout the novel Stafford juxtaposes young and old, present and past, Andrew and Katharine. Technically, as in *Boston Adventure*, the structure of the tightly built novel reinforces the theme, for its eight chapters, whose titles are ironic variations on "The Twelve Days of Christmas," alternate in focus and point of view between the young boy and his beautiful cousin.

Stafford's artistic advancements in *The Catherine Wheel* are accompanied—indeed facilitated—by a thematic coming-of-age. Although Andrew is a sensitive and sympathetic character, *The Catherine Wheel* is Katharine's novel. In Katharine Congreve, Stafford creates an adult hero, in whom Sonie Marburg and Molly Fawcett grow up. Stafford's attention to a mature protagonist announces not the end of her interest in the female *Bildungsroman* but the maturation of her fascination with the theme and form of the female novel of development.

Feminist critics and scholars, recognizing the diversity of the form, have identified two distinct narrative patterns in the female *Bildungsroman*—the traditional, essentially chronological, story of apprenticeship; and the awakening, the delayed development of the mature hero that is manifested most often in brief, epiphanic flashes of internal recognition. Just as *Boston Adventure* and *The Mountain Lion* contain many of the archetypal patterns evident in the female novel of apprenticeship, *The Catherine Wheel* exhibits many of the characteristics of the novel of awakening.

Although Katharine, a mature, independent woman, is (despite some similarities with Lucy Pride) a new type of character in Stafford's novels, her appearance in *The Catherine Wheel* is presaged by some of the author's earlier stories. Published in 1946, 1948, and 1950, respectively, "The Interior Castle," "Children Are Bored on Sunday," and "A Country Love Story," among others, present adult women who confront the circumstances of their lives essentially alone. The intelligent, sensitive woman who is—whether unmarried, widowed or divorced, or emotionally abandoned by a husband—living alone is a familiar Stafford character who appears throughout her oeuvre. The woman trying to live on her own, the woman who is "not half of a couple and fulfills no set function within a nuclear family," the so-called "odd-woman," is, according to Annis Pratt, an equally common figure throughout women's fiction.[2]

The single woman, having rejected or failed to attain marriage and family, has in the eyes of a patriarchal society avoided responsible womanhood and is therefore both suspect and eccentric. Denied the sanctioned sexual relationship of marriage, the single woman, whatever her choice about her sexuality, is disdained by society. "In a society that associates feminine sexuality with subordination to a male, both women who refuse permanent heterosexual relationships and women who choose celibacy are outcasts. The fact that freely undertaken sexual choices of any kind contradict patriarchal expectations for women accounts for the scorn heaped upon women who do *and* women who don't, sexually active and sexually celibate women alike."[3] Deprived of a viable role in society, single women in fiction find solace, much like their younger sisters, in nature. Echoing the Green-World Archetype, in which the adolescent girl strives to possess herself through a possession of nature, the adult single woman retreats from the disapproving world to the wholeness and serenity of nature.

Stafford's "odd-woman" hero, Katharine Congreve, is not the stereotypical unmarried woman. Neither bitter, unattractive spinster nor tough career woman, she is a beautiful, caring woman who, at thirty-nine, appears composed and content with her life. Like Lucy Pride's, Katharine's aristocratic, wealthy heritage renders her immune to the practical concerns of money and employment, and allows her to eschew a marriage that would offer financial security or social validity. Because in a patriarchal society, necessity notwithstanding, women are expected to marry, in her middle years Katharine's single status remains a puzzle to her friends and family: "The twins literally

2. Pratt, *Archetypal Patterns in Women's Fiction*, 113.
3. *Ibid.*, 119–20.

could spend hours speculating on why Cousin Katharine had never married. This was the darkest of all tribal mysteries and Andrew was sure that not even his mother knew the answer" (*CW*, 47–48). Katharine has had opportunities for marriage, and her charms have not abated with age. In the city she entertains her "'young men,' a retinue of dazzled youths who came in droves from Cambridge on her 'day' to be inspired to sonnet-writing by her beauty and her charm" (*CW*, 54). Her adoring young cousins and elderly neighbors concur that "every man in the world is in love with Katharine C" (*CW*, 61). The twins, Honor and Harriet, delight in Katharine's stories of old beaux and rejected proposals, and are convinced that their cousin has never married because "no one in the whole world was good enough for her" (*CW*, 48).

Her naïve devotees' conclusion is not altogether hyperbolic. To some extent no one *is* good enough for Katharine Congreve, who has remained, emotionally and morally, the innocent young woman who was at seventeen rejected by her only love, when he met and fell in love with her "uncertain poor relation," Maeve, her orphaned cousin, her friend and confidante. Some twenty years before the time of the novel, Maeve's return to Congreve House from a visit with an aunt coincides with Katharine's pledge to marry young John Shipley and her seventeenth birthday ball, held on a summer evening when "the whole natural world had seemed a background constructed for this one particular night in Katharine's history to accent and deepen her triumphant blossoming" (*CW*, 80). But Katharine is never to bloom, and while she faithfully endures her beloved's defection, "undetected, unsuspected, the cancer spread until its progress and its malevolent pain became the armature of her whole thought and conduct" (*CW*, 82). A brokenhearted Katharine steels herself willfully against the pain, and "after years and years of frugal living upon wreckage," at thirty-nine, she "who had never healed" remains unchanged: "But for her white hair, she was the same as she had been at nineteen when her lover had married someone else, at seventeen when she had sworn to marry him" (*CW*, 232, 77). Katharine's father, the only person ever to know of her thwarted love, consoles his daughter on the night of her loss: "Poor dear," he confides, "I had hoped for you there'd be no compromise" (*CW*, 83). The central fact of Katharine's life is that she does not compromise, and therefore does not change. Watching her beloved "Humanist" at his studies, the bereaved girl recognizes that "like her father, note-maker, student for study's sake, she would never participate, that she would read astutely and never write, observe wholeheartedly and never paint, not teach, not marry God. Untalented and uncompromising, she would not commit herself" (*CW*, 84).

Katharine, like Molly Fawcett, strives to remain an innocent, preserving in her iconoclastic, archaic life-style the world and emotions of her youth. "There is only one time," she tells her young cousins, "and that is the past time. There is no fashion in *now* or in *tomorrow* because the goods has not been cut" (*CW*, 43). Katharine, who believes that "the Dublin and the Rome where the elder Shipleys went each year were in every particular the cities she had known as a girl and had not revisited for eighteen years," insists upon the preservation of her life as it was before her heart was broken (*CW*, 43). For her, "There was no progression in time because there was no perspective and therefore no shrouding of the past; the present was exactly the same size as the past and of exactly the same importance and except in the most minor and mechanical of ways, the future did not seem to exist" (*CW*, 44).

However naïve, Katharine is a sensitive, intelligent woman who knows that the price of her immutability is her inability to participate in the world. An observer of life, she cannot paint, teach, marry God—cannot, in fact, marry at all. When a pitifully distraught John Shipley returns to her, insistent that "they must save him, together, *no matter what*," Katharine's conditional agreement brings a recognition of the now-inevitable adult compromise: "She was an honest woman with herself and did not beat around the bush: she was and had always been 'in love' with John Shipley and she did not love him and she knew that at the moment of conjugal commitment, the state of being in love would be annulled and she would never be accessible to him again through any ruse" (*CW*, 92, 94). Later in the summer, another old beau, Edmund St. Denis, visits Congreve House with his wife and son and, in a "gross and platitudinous burlesque of John Shipley's protestations," announces to Katharine that she should have married him. "You are a wonder, Kate," he marvels, "You haven't changed at all." Katharine replies, "*Not* changing is my only occupation. . . . But if I had married, then I might have changed and changed in a way you wouldn't have liked" (*CW*, 174, 173). Certainly, for Katharine, marriage would have meant change—change in a way she wouldn't have liked.

Katharine's rejection of marriage is precipitated by her shame and despair at John Shipley's abjuration, but as she recognizes, her decision to remain single has contributed to her development as a strong, independent woman. Only single could Katharine have matured into the woman that she is. Although Stafford ultimately, as always, rejects her protagonist's isolation, she nonetheless demonstrates, in her creation of Katharine Congreve, her belief in the validity of the woman alone, and her inheritance of the feminine literary tradition. As Annis Pratt notes, "In literature dealing with single women . . . authors seem to be clearing out a new space that is in actuality an old, or archetypal, landscape of the psyche, a place that, essentially apatriarchal, contains once-forgotten possibilities of personal development." Yet, while marriage may stultify a woman's quest for selfhood and authenticity, a repudiation of marriage does not imply a rejection of all human interaction. As Heather McClave writes in her introduction to *Women Writers of the Short Story*, female writers share a belief that self-knowledge is achieved through one's relationship with others. Pratt affirms—and Stafford reaffirms—that though "'keeping your shape' seems to be easier in the single state than in marriage . . . modern single women heroes . . . do not always achieve this state by avoiding personal relationships, but, more often, by seeing them as a step towards the ultimate goal of selfhood." Classic modern single female heroes "are likely to continue in their quests for love and for human relationships while protecting their solitary selves from excessive ravishment."[4]

Katharine Congreve, despite her lingering pain and her puritanic belief that she has "never learned to demonstrate," is a caring, loving woman (*CW*, 68). At seventeen, devastated by her recognition that John Shipley does not love her, she nonetheless reaffirms her love for him and her cousin when he, imagining "that she had deliberately brought them together," proposes to her, "their ambassadress . . . that the three of them be a triumvirate for life" (*CW*, 83). Katharine accompanies the young couple on their European honeymoon and

4. *Ibid.*, 127; Heather McClave, Introduction to *Women Writers of the Short Story* (Englewood Cliffs, N.J., 1980), 4; Pratt, *Archetypal Patterns in Women's Fiction*, 127, 128.

throughout the years remains their friend: "This indivisible trinity, established long before Maeve and John were married, was looked on as the most winning friendship in Boston. . . . Such was their community that they gave the impression of being three aspects of the same person and not three separate persons" (*CW*, 54). The relationship is important to Katharine, but painful. As John Shipley's "second wife" and Maeve's "second self," she is a secondary person, subordinating her heartache to the needs of these weaker, dependent friends.

Even needier are Andrew, Honor, and Harriet, the unhappy adolescents who, this year, confused by the ambience of misery that hovers about their household, have "individually sought consolation" in their beloved cousin (*CW*, 20). Katharine loves the children, who are themselves her consolation: "No one should ever know except herself the envy that had grated on her when she had learned that Maeve was pregnant" (*CW*, 156). And they adore her, their friend and their confessor, "their sponsor, playmate, teacher, second mother" (*CW*, 52). That Katharine is a better mother than Maeve, a "rather vague, somehow always slightly worried, rather humble, faintly discouraging woman," whom Andrew finds so wanting in comparison to her sensitive friend, is a bitter irony (*CW*, 201). Katharine's close relationship with and time for the children are a function of her independence. Maeve, "in every particular a constant wife," faithfully accompanies her husband on his annual junkets to Europe, even though she confides to Katharine that she would rather join her children at Congreve House. For a somewhat selfish Katharine, however, the summer "arrangement could not have been more felicitous; Congreve House was too big for her by herself, she loved the children and they loved her" (*CW*, 90–91).

The Shipley children's affection for Katharine is shared by her neighbors, the elderly, eccentric residents of Hawthorne for whom she is "the world around which all lesser worlds revolved" (*CW*, 51). Her inevitable annual return to passé Hawthorne, her generous charity, and her old-fashioned elegance endear her to the citizenry, who adore and fuss over their "own Empress Katharine" like grateful peasants attending a benevolent queen (*CW*, 107). A comic entourage, they are typically Staffordian freaks: dirty, toothless Em Bugtown begs food and silver spoons from her neighbors, epileptic Jasper has fits in the center of town, and the "fabulously corpulent Bluebell

James . . . had had a bastard baby every year since she was twelve"
(*CW*, 110–111). Katharine's immediate circle includes the no-nonsense
New Englander, laconic Peg Duff, in her mechanic's overall and base-
ball cap; perennially happy Mr. Barker; and pleasant, wheelchair-
bound Miss Celia Heminway. All of them—except Em Bugtown, who
declares portentously that "Lady Katharine" will pay for her name-
less "black sins"—idolize their wealthy patroness, and when her bedroom light announces to Hawthorne that Katharine has spent a sleepless night, the town buzzes all the following day with conjecture and
concern about Andrew's "rich and beautiful maiden cousin" (*CW*, 108).
Katharine reciprocates her friends' affection. At the party celebrat-
ing the St. Denises' midsummer visit, she observes her "ancient play-
mates" and thinks "how extremely pleasant her life of compromise
among them all was and how extremely careless it would be to give it
up and go to live [with John Shipley]. . . . She could not leave any of
them" (*CW*, 164–165).

A queen cannot abandon her loyal subjects; a loving mother will not
leave her children. Katharine knows that she is indispensable to the
people in her life, and, nurturing, caring, quintessentially feminine,
she cannot sacrifice them to the appeals of John Shipley or even to the
possibilities for her own happiness. Yet, if Katharine is central to her
society, she is nonetheless both regal and independent, not *of* it. To
some extent Katharine is the most freakish of all the characters,
taking on in her solitary strength extra-human characteristics.

Andrew is genuinely puzzled by his cousin's sleepless night, for although he cannot imagine what she could have been doing in her room
all night, he is certain that "Cousin Katharine was above sickness except for the flu occasionally when there was an epidemic" (*CW*, 106).
Katharine is, it seems, above human frailty. Her unusual behavior
and Andrew's perduring boredom inspire the boy to new perceptions
about his favorite adult.

> When he came to think of it, Cousin Katharine was awfully peculiar; he
> had always before taken her for granted but suddenly he no longer did.
> Why, for example, was she so attached to such old-fashioned pastimes?
> The game of patience while she drank her tea if she had no visitors; the
> simple needle-point; the making of potpourri with sun-dried rose petals;
> the outmoded customs of reading poetry aloud, and mounting butter-
> flies on pins. She even smelled old-fashioned, of some fastidious, coun-
> trified scent (Maddox [the gardener] made it for her from an arcane re-

ceipt) no more nameable than the general sweetness of a rural garden just come into bloom. She moved in a nebula of this and of dove-gray chiffon or lilac lawn, regarding the works of Robert Browning and the Roman poets through a shell lorgnette or watching the birds which she described in a black ledger with a thin gold pencil, rejoicing in them all except for the puffin which she found absurd and the cowbird which she deplored on moral grounds. The cat was always doomed from kittenhood to wear a bell of piercing tone. (*CW*, 131)

Enduring and mysterious, Katharine is also unusually perceptive. Andrew's bitterness at his friend's betrayal intensifies in his lingering, lonely hours, and sensing that his cousin has intuited his silent prayers for Charles Smithwick's death, he comes to fear her superhuman powers: "He knew that Cousin Katharine knew everything. Her eyes were inescapable" (*CW*, 151).

Although much of what we learn about Katharine is from troubled, innocent—and therefore not always reliable—Andrew, other characters' perceptions and his cousin's own actions reinforce the boy's impression that Katharine is special and unusual, as does Stafford's employment in *The Catherine Wheel* of the feminine literary tradition. Society's fear of the "powerful, untrammeled woman who, by daring to *enjoy* her unmarried state, defies social norms," Pratt observes, often earns her the label of "witch": "The old maid is frequently associated in popular culture with the witch, the two stereotypes springing from a common gynophobic fear of self-determined women." The witch, according to Mary Daly in *Beyond God the Father*, is often associated with the wise woman who knows how to cure with herbs and who offers advice and counsel to her neighbors.[5] In *The Catherine Wheel*, the stereotypical wise woman is the widowed Beulah Smithwick, the mother of Andrew's friend Victor and a "sly and frowsy necromancer who could foresee the future and disclose the past in a pack of filthy playing cards or a pattern of wet tea-leaves" (*CW*, 111). Katharine, though too civilized and sophisticated to exhibit the eccentric behavior of Mrs. Smithwick, shares her neighbor's curious powers. She tells her own fortune with tarot cards and, "continuing the mythology as an essential part of Congreve House," sustains her father's belief that the house is haunted by "an august body of ghosts" named for characters from the novels of Thomas Hardy (*CW*, 163). Kath-

5. Pratt, *Archetypal Patterns in Women's Fiction*, 122–23; Mary Daly, *Beyond God the Father: Toward a Philosophy of Women's Liberation* (Boston, 1973).

arine's eccentricity is confirmed late in the novel when she does "the queerest thing of her whole life," according to Andrew; she commissions and designs her own tombstone (*CW*, 185). Her beloved Mr. Barker's explanation for the fact that the "gardens of Congreve House are a veritable paradise" is that "this seemingly good Christian woman says incantations when the moon is full and does her plantin' when the Widow Smithwick's crystal ball gives her the go-ahead sign" (*CW*, 157).

Mr. Barker's humor aside, Katharine's veneration of Congreve House, her father's legacy and the scene of her childhood joys and her adolescent betrayal, is a salient aspect of her personality. Recognizing that she is not really content anywhere except Congreve House, Katharine savors its sensuous enchantments: "Serenity ripened in her face and she parted her lips in a fond smile, cherishing everything she surveyed and smelled and heard, the dimming medallions of the wallpaper and the Audubon prints that ascended the wall; the commingled fragrances of sunning foliage and old, oiled furniture and flowers everywhere, within the house and out, all bound together by the fresh salt breeze, a constant wraith in the curtains, a perpetual touch, feather-light and tentative, on the pages of open books and the tassels of velvet table covers; the multitudinous bird-song, the far-off bells of buoys" (*CW*, 61–62). Katharine's summer retreat to Congreve House is a return to nature, to the "orchards and gardens and acres of lawn" that encircle the large white house (*CW*, 62). From the house, the mistress can survey her luxurious grounds.

> The long, embrasured windows of the house commanded, at the back, a view of the wide blue lake ringed with thin pines that cast their Oriental images blackly over the waving water. From the drawing room and the dining room, one looked out on the green swirl of the tidal river, spangled with the silver wings of gulls and the white pouches of spinnakers. From the east windows and those on the west, Katharine looked toward meadows, magisterial and vast, two oval yellow seas bounded by black country lanes. Beyond the western meadow there was a dense blue forest where the sun could never penetrate and where there always hung a gun-blue haze between the trees, where, in certain places, there were dells as green as Ireland and the mossy earth was bejeweled with monkshood and blue-bells. (*CW*, 63)

Throughout *The Catherine Wheel* Katharine interacts with the natural world. A typical summer at Congreve House boasts daily picnics, swimming, rowing on the lake, the selection and arrangement of flowers. Most of Katharine's entertaining at Congreve House is conducted in the open air—tea on the lawn, formal balls on a platform festooned with crepe-paper lanterns. The crucial event of her life, John Shipley's rejection of her for Maeve, occurs at her alfresco seventeenth birthday ball; the idyllic setting of Congreve House "furthered—even created" the romance of John and Maeve, and in their boundless love they reach out to embrace Katharine (*CW*, 83). Honor and Harriet find Cousin Katharine's trip to Europe with the Shipleys on their honeymoon "so debonair, so airy and jocose" that they raise the subject whenever they can, and in Katharine's stories to the children about her travels with their parents, the memorable events seem invariably to have occurred outdoors (*CW*, 45).

Katharine's delight in the natural world reinforces her preternatural characteristics. As Pratt writes:

> Witchcraft, a Stone Age religion in which the priestess plays the role of the goddess and in which the sun and moon, seasonal cycles, birth, fertility, and vegetation are the focus of the rituals, belongs to the green-world archetype; it is a set of practices and beliefs linking women to nature. Even when authors are not explicitly (or perhaps even consciously) dealing with witches as such, fiction in which heroes draw power for self-sufficiency from nature has perennially delighted the reading audience. . . . Women heroes are described as laws unto themselves in their solitude, happy among the animals and plants, sometimes in the company of other women but essentially alone.

Katharine Congreve's delight in nature is, like Molly Fawcett's retreat to her mountain study, an enactment of the Green-World Archetype in women's fiction. Whereas the escape to nature is for the adolescent hero sometimes a temporary respite that prepares her to interact with the outside world, more often in the novel of awakening a lifelong allegiance to nature is the mature female hero's demonstration and protestation that the patriarchal culture will not allow women to become themselves: "Both the girl's desire and society's discouragement are reflected in women's fiction, where, as a result, nature for the young hero remains a refuge throughout life."[6] Stafford creates in Katharine Congreve a protagonist whose discovery of psychological sustenance in the natural world allows her to develop into a mature, independent hero.

6. Pratt, *Archetypal Patterns in Women's Fiction*, 125, 17.

In *The Catherine Wheel*, as in much women's fiction, the female hero's devotion to the green world combines with her reliance on interpersonal relationships to lead her to a broader psychological realm. "For all these older women heroes," remarks Pratt, "the road towards self-understanding that they had previously pursued—namely, relationships with other people—becomes increasingly secondary, giving way to a puzzling over the nature of the cosmos itself rather than over human entanglements. . . . At the same time, the quest for the pulse of nature is attuned to something 'spiritual,' the beloved green world providing a bridge to the wider universe." While in the novel of development, the goal of the young hero is integration within a community, in the novel of awakening, the mature protagonist's quest is most often a journey within: "Her goal is to integrate her self with herself and not with a society she has found inimical to her desires."[7] In middle age, with John Shipley's proposal, Katharine Congreve is compelled to analyze her personal relationships and her life-style, and to undertake her journey into her "interior castle." Katharine's rebirth journey echoes the quest into the unconscious undertaken by mature female heroes throughout women's fiction.

In *Archetypal Patterns in Women's Fiction*, Pratt offers a revisionist interpretation of Carl Jung's theory of the transformation, or "individuation," process, in which the individual's descent into the unconscious results in a renewal of self. In Phase I of the woman's rebirth journey, the "splitting off from family, husbands, lovers," the hero, according to Pratt, experiences "an acute consciousness of the world of the ego and of a consequent turning away from societal norms."[8] In *The Catherine Wheel*, Katharine's introspection is first perceived by Andrew, who is distressed by his cousin's apparent lack of interest in his well-being: "Cousin Katharine had appeared not to notice his despair and this astonished him because she had always before sensed his troubles and had done what she could to ease them" (*CW*, 25). Andrew does not know, and the reader does not learn until the second chapter and the shift in the novel to Katharine's point of view, that Katharine's move away from her sensitive young cousin is a result of her turning within and her consideration of his father's proposition that she "sell Congreve House, leave Boston and go with him to

7. *Ibid.*, 129–30, 136.
8. *Ibid.*, 139.

'begin again' in some outpost of the earth" (*CW*, 93). Shipley's proposal and Katharine's contemplation of a rejection of her socially acceptable life-style precipitate her journey into the unconscious, which is further facilitated by her relationship with nature.

In Phase II of the quest, a green-world guide or token, commonly an ordinary object or phenomenon that assumes portentous significance, emerges (often in esoteric form) to urge the hero toward her journey. The token, as well as the green-world lover, who appears in the next phase of the quest, seems "matrilinear in the general sense of suggesting a realm of inherited feminine power quite different from patriarchal culture."[9] Several symbols, each in some form feminine, function in Katharine's psychic quest, most notably the Catherine wheel, one of the major symbols in the novel, which becomes increasingly central as Katherine undertakes her interior journey. It is in the light of that firework, which "revolved insanely on its separate planes of scarlet and green, sizzling and thundering as the wild spokes fired each other," that seventeen-year-old Katharine, turning in "an ecstasy" to her lover, perceives that he does not love her (*CW*, 82). Katharine's discovery fixes her upon "the spinning rack" of her own lifelong Catherine wheel, and as she plans her final summer's commemorative ball, with dancing, champagne, and "the chief thing . . . fireworks," she orders a pyrotechnical display with a preponderance of Catherine wheels (*CW*, 148, 156). The finale of the highlight of the ball is to be five Catherine wheels, set off by Andrew; Maddox, the gardener; and Charles Smithwick; but the final Catherine wheel is a dud, and it is Katharine who rushes to aid burning Charles, Katharine whose diaphanous white dress catches fire and who, panicking, runs—like the Catherine wheel—in a "widening circle," fanning the fatal flames (*CW*, 279). Her dying words are for Andrew: "I heard the Catherine wheel swinging low to get me . . . only it swung high, it swung, it swung, it swung" (*CW*, 280).

The Catherine wheel is associated too with Katharine's tombstone, another of the nature tokens in the novel, insofar as death involves the return to the earth of the body. She commissions the tombstone late in the novel, perplexing her friends and provoking Andrew to wonder whether "she did have some knowledge of her death, told her

9. *Ibid.*, 141.

in a dream" (*CW*, 187). The tombstone is custom-designed and recreates Katharine with "her protuberant pompadour arising from her wide forehead and her noble nose and chin and her broad, loving lips, but it showed, even more wonderfully, her pure and vestal air" (*CW*, 236). Above her head is a Catherine wheel, a carved circle with inward-curving spikes, the symbol, Katharine explains, of the martyr Catherine. The fourth-century saint Catherine of Alexandria, a virgin of patrician heritage who, after persuading the empress to become a Christian, was tortured upon the rack of the Catherine wheel, was decapitated after the wheel broke before killing her. The patron of maidens and philosophers, Catherine is commonly portrayed with a book and a crown to signify her learning and her noble birth. Her virginity, nobility, and learning associate the martyr with Katharine, much to her friends' dismay. "That's too far-fetched for words," pronounces Mrs. Wainwright-Lowe after Katharine's explanation of the tombstone motif. "Whoever in the world scourged you?" (*CW*, 239). Katharine confides to her diary her private motivation for the reminder of her mortality: "It is a kind of insurance—however tenuous and symbolic—against my suddenly kicking over the traces and going off to a flamboyant island in my middle age" (*CW*, 217). But Andrew is convinced that the stone is a sign, that with its delivery something momentous will occur. At the novel's denouement, he watches in terror as the "quick, ravishing wheel" consumes his cousin, "while in the stable her other one, motionless in stone, was as cool and as permanent as the sky. Andrew had been right, after all: her tombstone was a sign" (*CW*, 278).

Like the Catherine wheel and the tombstone, an inanimate object comes alive with significance to accompany Katharine in Phase III of her journey, the phase that Pratt terms the "Green-World Lover." Pratt states, "Whether as an ideal figure or a revery one, an ideal, nonpatriarchal lover sometimes appears as an initiatory guide and often aids at difficult points in the quest. He (sometimes she or it) does not constitute the turning point or goal of the rebirth journey, as does the goddess or anima in the male rebirth journey . . . [but] leads the hero away from society and towards her own unconscious depths." Katharine, who works sporadically at a needlepoint depiction of a unicorn and a virgin, is associated with the unicorn that appears in women's poetry and needlework and often functions as a green-world lover.[10] But her green-world lover is the Roman goddess Minerva, a statue of whom "stood in a summerhouse at the end of the pergola which her father had made as a present to her on her fifteenth birthday, astonishing everyone who had imagined that, like other girls, she would have preferred necklaces or frocks" (*CW*, 67). At seventeen, recognizing her love, Katharine had prostrated herself to Minerva, "the protectress assigned to her by her learning-loving father," and had vowed to marry John Shipley (*CW*, 77–78). The temple of Katharine's virgin protectress, the scene of outdoor lunches and midafternoon birch-beer respites, is, like Katharine herself, an integral component of Congreve House. And Katharine identifies with Minerva, the blue-eyed goddess of wisdom, war, and the liberal arts, a miniature version of whom graces her bedroom table. Andrew recognizes the alliance between his cousin and her goddess and their appropriateness at Congreve House. Gazing at Katharine from his hammock as she stops at the front door to listen to a bird's song, the boy notices that "she . . . so motionless and so tall . . . looked to be a part of the house itself, like the cool, impassive statue of Minerva" (*CW*, 128). And, observing her likeness on the tombstone, which was carved by the stonecutter who had crafted the Minerva some twenty-five years earlier, he notes that the "marble effigy" is "as heroic and as handsome" as the statue of Minerva (*CW*, 236). Katharine's tombstone will rest behind Minerva's temple, under the fig tree that shades the grave of her father.

In the "Confrontation with Parental Figures," Phase IV of the rebirth journey, the mature hero, unlike the young woman who engages in a real battle, confronts figures from the past and is reconciled with "the father and mother figures resident in . . . the subconscious, her repository of personal memories."[11] For the single woman, whose parental dependencies and loyalties have not been supplanted in maturity by the emotional claims of a husband and children, one would expect that the parents are often particularly salient figures. Yet, like Minerva, who was born from Jupiter's brain full-grown and armed, Katharine is in every practical sense motherless. Her mother, who is barely mentioned in *The Catherine Wheel*, has "nothing at all in common with her daughter" (*CW*, 85). "As Progressive as

10. *Ibid.*, 140.
11. *Ibid.*

Katharine was Conservative," she is an active, committed woman, "a Baconian, an anti-vivisectionist, an advocate of butter-milk and rat control," a woman whose unhappy marriage and dissimilarity to her introspective, intellectual husband and daughter have relegated her to a minor role in their lives and in the novel (*CW*, 62). But if her mother's significance in Katharine's life is negligible, the centrality of her father in her life is notable. Again like Minerva, who was one of Jupiter's most faithful counselors and, in fact, the only divinity whose authority equaled her father's, Katharine long after her father's death both enjoys and is emburdened by her deep feelings for her male parent.

Like many of Jean Stafford's female characters—including Molly Fawcett, Mrs. Fawcett, Sonie Marburg, and, most obviously, Lucy Pride—Katharine idolizes her father. Soon after her appearance as the point-of-view character in the second chapter of the novel, she slowly climbs the stairs to her sitting room, stopping, as is her daily habit, to peruse the portrait of her father that hangs at the head of the stairs. "Renew[ing] her memory" of the strong, proud face from whose hers, "softened to a female role," is derived, she muses upon the resoluteness that the two share.

> These fine long faces were civilized. They were the faces of people so endowed with control and tact and insight and second sight that the feelings that might in secret ravage the spirit could never take the battlements of the flesh; no undue passion would ever show in those prudent eyes or on those discreet and handsome lips. For there was no doubt here, no self-contempt, but only the imposing courage of sterling good looks and the protecting lucidity of charm. So compelling was the integrity and the impregnable, intelligent self-respect that as Katharine looked at the masterful painted face, her source and counterpart, euphoria at her good luck extended her height and the length of her narrow hands and narrow feet and she felt as heroically proportioned as the statue of Minerva. (*CW*, 66–67)

Like Lucy Pride, Katharine preserves her father's domain as it existed during his lifetime. Her commitment to the past and old-fashioned mores is not so much quaint eccentricity as an attempt to guarantee that the customs in Congreve House remain the same as they had been in her father's day. Her boundless love and respect for "the Humanist" notwithstanding, however, Katharine is not blind to her father's faults. She has known since her adolescence that her parents' marriage was unhappy, that her father had a mistress, and that he had often appeared to prefer Maeve to his own daughter because "Maeve was not the daughter of his wife whom he did not love" (*CW*, 214). Although later, "when he grew accustomed to his guilt," her father had begun to favor Katharine, her childhood jealousy of her cousin still rankles (*CW*, 213–214). From her father, Katharine is aware that she has inherited her inability to participate, her ascetic, intellectual, uninvolved approach to life. And yet, ultimately, her father is the stabilizer and the single love of Katharine's life. Only he makes tolerable the presence of Maeve and John after the latter's rejection of Katharine. Late in the novel, tortured by another inexplicable sleepless night, she "call[s] off the roll of the men who had been in love with her as, in gentle lamplight, she gazed at herself in the mirror, drowning in her beauty; stripped of every amenity, enthroned upon her invincible self-love, she would fall forward on her arms without any warning, her realm sacked, her sovereignty dissolved and weep and weep and weep and with her wet lips pressed to the back of her hand, murmur, 'They did not. Only the Humanist loved me'" (*CW*, 231).

In her beloved father Katharine finds strength and sustenance. Toward the end of *The Catherine Wheel,* as she prepares to make her appearance at the ball that ends the novel, she berates herself for her emotional upheaval and, looking at her father's portrait, is "ashamed, meeting the face in which judgement and resignation were balanced equally. As if he were there and had held her up to friendly ridicule, had said all this emotion was infantile and unattractive, she felt her broken structure begin to mend, begin to move articulately, and whole, mistress of Congreve House, she emerged from the embrace of it into the summer evening" (*CW*, 265–266).

Katharine may feel complete and in control as she prepares to preside at her end-of-summer celebration, but the novel's denouement proves otherwise. Katharine's fate conforms to the conventions of the rebirth journey, in which Phase V, the "Plunge into the Unconscious," the final phase of the quest, culminates in the female hero's rebirth or in her destruction. According to Pratt, after the female hero confronts the figures of her subconscious, she is ready to journey to the unconscious. In Jung's conception of the rebirth journey, at this phase, in which the hero confronts the "shadow" in the unconscious, it is socially rebellious. "In women's fiction, quite the contrary, the shadow seems to bring with it from the social world the opprobrium for womanhood associated with sexism, infusing characters with self-loathing. Women heroes often blame themselves for their own normal human desires. . . . For women, the shadow of self-hatred is tremendously strengthened by complicity with society." In the male journey, the shadow merges with the anima, the confrontation with which is the "crucial experience leading the male back to society as a superordinate or reborn person," but in the female journey, the shadow combines with the animus to block the hero's complete development. Unless the hero is able to overcome the animus to discover her feminine power, she is likely to become the victim of a thwarted journey or to be punished by the patriarchal society that cannot accept her powerful, transformed persona. Such fates "may account for the greater number of novels in which women are done to death or driven mad by their socially acceptable consorts than of novels in which they achieve rebirth."[12]

Katharine Congreve's plunge into the unconscious begins early in the novel, with her memory of her reaction to her agreement to flee society with middle-aged, forlorn John Shipley. The descent is associated with sleeplessness and death. Plagued by insomnia, Katharine takes a sleeping pill, and "as the medicine began to solace her and she began to descend circuitously and slowly like a leaf falling to earth in a demure breeze, she wished, not thinking of John or Maeve or of the children but only of herself, never to awaken. For the first time in her life, she thought of life's alternative as delectable; with her whole heart she wished to die" (*CW*, 94). The next afternoon, when Andrew visits and artlessly mentions Mangareva, the outpost that Katharine and his father have chosen to flee to, Katharine's guilt and her fear that the boy has intuited their plans provoke another "blinding, dumbing annihilation of reality" upon the "wrenching rack" of her own Catherine wheel (*CW*, 96). Later, once again "swept upward, outward and pressed down by" one of her mysterious trances, she considers her startling behavior in the pages of her diary.

> Poor, lonely obsessed Katharine. For I am snatched by moments of hallucination when reality disgorges me like a cannon firing off a can-

12. *Ibid.*, 141, 142.

non ball and I am sent off into an upper air where there is no sound
and my senses are destroyed by the awful, white, paining light. I know
that it is only a matter of seconds because there (wherever *there* may
be) time does not exist, it is also eternity, unchanging, looking forward
to no equinox, no winter, no spring, no day. Upon a matter so indefi-
nite, having no attendant symptoms, no preamble, no pattern of any
kind, I can consult no one. What or whom do I serve? Solomon himself
could not tell me. . . . If fear or regret attended it or any other vapor-
ing from a tangible cause, I could find the proper physic for myself.
But there is no fear except the fear within the experience itself which
is, to be sure, a fear of the utmost intensity: it is ideal and has no object that I can name. At the same time that I rise, ejected from the
planet into the empyrean, I plummet through the core of the world.
(*CW*, 74–75)

Katharine recognizes, then, that her illness is not physiological, and
for the strong-willed, indomitable woman, the thought of an emotional or mental malady is even more upsetting: "She could not bear
to think that any fiber of her will could relax and she was afraid it had
already begun to happen and that the ganglion of her being was beginning, slowly, to atrophy" (*CW*, 156).

Katharine unconsciously perceives that the weakening of her will
will result in—indeed necessitate—her death. Noting the twins' innocent enjoyment of a midsummer party, their naïve luxuriating in
the time "before the intimations of one's immortality had ceased," she
finds herself welcoming her disturbing state of mind, "finding in it
. . . a certain excitement and even an attractiveness like something
romantically forbidden, like certain kinds of pain that one should not
enjoy but did—opium-eating perhaps, that imperiled the spirit but
quelled the pain" (*CW*, 160). Temporarily intrigued by her aberrations, she wonders what her friends would think of her secret "nightmare": "Not one of them guesses that I have had glimpses of a morbid
world hidden beneath my reason and my senses." And the morbid
world, she decides, resembles "her conception of death" (*CW*, 161, 160).

The next occurrence of the revolving trance is inspired by Andrew
and Katharine's fear that he has rejected her. This time, as "the
wheel began, in the dark vault of her heart, slowly to revolve," the
experience has sexual overtones. Katharine, "terrorized and longing
for the climax of her terror," knows "that her longing was obscene."
And, just as Sonie tries to govern the red room, she struggles to

control the "dislocation": "She disciplined herself, she could stop the wheel" (*CW*, 161). Her indomitability is short-lived, however, for the unexpected and pitiful proposal from Edmund St. Denis evokes another trance: "Green clouds rose, layer after layer, for the sun-like Catherine wheel, the absolute, unburying itself and edging up behind the dogs' backs of tremendous waves. The inseparable mind sang in its bone-cell and she was wheeled outward swiftly and the purblind mind nosed like a mole through splendid mansions of ice-white bone and luminous blood, singing with the music of the spheres" (*CW*, 175–176).

Despite Katharine's resistance to her interior journey, and her efforts to intellectualize and overcome its effects, her unconscious begins to prevail. Again, with an as yet incomplete knowledge of her death, she perceives the pervasiveness of her dissolution: "My life is seeping out of me, she thought, the nightmare vitiates my charm" (*CW*, 97). And when, although she has not cried since Shipley's betrayal, she tries to cry in response to a prank of Andrew's that frightens her, she discovers that "even in her extremity she could not seduce a single tear from her eyes. She had misplaced her rose-colored glasses which until now had taken the place of the gift of tears, and because she was herself bedeviled without them, she saw in everyone the symptoms of decay" (*CW*, 212). Another trivial incident reminds her that "at another time in her life, Katharine Congreve, who believed in sweetness and light and the superfluity of all else, would have refused to remember it. . . . But 'at another time in her life' she had not yet opened up Pandora's box" (*CW*, 221–222). Eventually Katharine begins to feel that "she was living in a void and that she would continue to for the rest of time with an occasional swift trip to chaos, changing the climate from despair to dementia" (*CW*, 216–217).

Still, Katharine hopes that she will recover from her "chimeral fancies"; that her attempt to write out her fears in her diary, which in six weeks has doubled in size, will cure her; that she can believe "the promise her reason made her, that there *had* to be an end to this sickness that alternated between coma and paroxysm, and that when the time came, her whole life might swing into a different course. . . . She, who had been constant, might change, but into what and through what means she could not yet imagine" (*CW*, 232). One indication of her expectations of change, she decides, will be a symbolic cremation, after the ball, of her diary, the "testimony of her years and years of living upon wreckage" (*CW*, 232).

But, unlike Sonie Marburg and like Molly Fawcett, an arrogant innocent who cannot change, or accept the inevitability of change and dissolution, Katharine will not transcend her guilt and doubts. Thinking about the children, "these three innocents whom she deeply loved, she travailed as she considered what they would become, tarnished with compromise, becalmed by convention" (*CW*, 73). Finally, still unable to compromise, Katharine accepts that she will not change: "The party, after all, thought Katharine, was not for her and the cremation of her regrets. . . . While she intended still to burn her diary . . . she did not expect to arise from the ashes of it; the act was far more expedient than symbolic . . . for, uncertain of the course her life was now to take, she did not want to leave behind these lares to be rummaged through" (*CW*, 258). When Katharine again seems to intuit her impending death, she characteristically resists the awareness, instead finding strength and solace in a sense of place: "Perfect and plenteous, Congreve House was the locus but was also the extension of herself; not the events that had taken place in it which she had clung to out of her stubborn self-destruction, but the very paneled walls themselves and the wide random boards of the floors and the marble mantels and, above all, the ironic spirit of the house, mature (as she must learn to be) and indestructible (as she was despite all her efforts to destroy herself)" (*CW*, 265). Reinforced by her affinity for Congreve House, and made whole in response to her father's imagined ridicule, Katharine appears at her ball, proclaiming to everyone that she has never been happier.

Jean Stafford recognizes and throughout her work demonstrates that the retreat to the interior castle is both alluring and perilous. Katharine's interior journey is repeated by women characters throughout Stafford's short stories, but only in this expansive treatment does the inner quest duplicate the traditional female pattern outlined by Pratt. Katharine's journey is unsuccessful and results in her death because she is unable to overcome her guilt over her lifelong resentment of Maeve and over her proposed affair with John; her final words are spoken to herself: "He was not worth it" (*CW*, 281). But the real reason for Katharine's death is even more fundamental; in Stafford's world the unforgivable sin is the refusal to interact, to grow, to risk. Molly's death is metaphorically necessary because she jeopardizes Ralph's maturity as a male; it is no less ineluctable because a child like Molly cannot survive in the real world: she must change or she must die. Similarly, Katharine's refusal to change and compromise necessitates her extinction.

IV
A World Unfit for
Solitary Living
The Short Stories

Although Jean Stafford's novels disclose her technical and thematic diversity, Stafford is more widely known as a short-story writer, and it is within the genre of the short story that she reached her artistic maturity. Between 1939 and 1978 she published forty-six stories, and for the last twenty-five years of her career her fiction was entirely in this form. It is in the stories that Stafford presents most vividly her alienated and joyless characters—a monstrously obese college student whose pathetic creation of a beautiful twin sister manifests her tragic psychosis; an orphaned Indian boy who is banished to a foreboding institution for the unwanted; a bored young woman who retreats from her husband's indifference into the solace of a mythical lover; a self-proclaimed rube who takes her first tentative steps toward recovery from a mental breakdown. Although the characters in Jean Stafford's short stories—the aged, the infirm, the crazy, the lost, women and children—are universal, they, like their counterparts in the novels, are defined by their Americanness and a communal postwar American experience. Perhaps the relatively greater success of her short stories can be attributed to Stafford's affinity for this inherently American genre.

In his study of the American short story, William Peden declares that the short story is the only major American literary form, and the only form in which Americans have always excelled. Ray B. West, Jr., in *The Short Story in America, 1900–1950*, identifies Washington Irving, Edgar Allan Poe, Hawthorne, and Melville as early theorists and practitioners of the short story and reaffirms that it is a distinctly American form. Peden maintains, further, that of all contemporary arts, the short story is the most sensitive to change in the social, moral, and political climate, and that postwar skepticism and the belief that the American dream of progress and order had been betrayed resulted in the "somberness of tone and seriousness of purpose" of the short fiction of the postwar period. This modern sensibility only underscores the dissatisfaction and alienation that, among others, Alfred Kazin identifies, in *On Native Grounds*, as endemic in all American literature.[1]

While Jean Stafford's American subjects and sensibility undoubtedly account in part for her success with the short-story form, there is as well a more formal explanation for her affinity for the genre. As Peden notes, the short story is particularly compatible with the fragmentary nature of modern life, and Stafford's ironic vision, her belief in the fundamental incongruity and incomprehensibility of life, no doubt made the short story particularly attractive to her. In *Radical Innocence*, Ihab Hassan remarks upon the peculiarly modernist orientation of the modern short story: "The rifeness of the novelette and short story is thus seen not merely as evidence of our frenetic and accelerated mode of existence, and of all the distractions created by our mass media. That rifeness is evidence, on a more basic level, that our lives can take shape only in sudden epiphanies or isolated moments of crisis, and that, indeed, since our world may come to an end without notice, we lack those powers of anticipation and development which longer novels imply."[2]

If her American literary heritage and ironic vision inclined Stafford toward the short-story form, her sexual heritage was undoubtedly influential too. Sandra M. Gilbert and Susan Gubar, in their important

1. William Peden, *The American Short Story* (Boston, 1964), 1; Ray B. West, Jr., *The Short Story in America, 1900–1950* (Chicago, 1952), 38; Kazin, *On Native Grounds*, 14.
2. Ihab Hassan, *Radical Innocence* (Princeton, N.J., 1961), 102.

study of the nineteenth-century woman writer, *The Madwoman in the Attic*, contend that females suffer from a peculiarly feminine "anxiety of authorship" that silences some potential writers, motivates some writers (Emily Dickinson, for example) not to publish their work, and inspires others (like Jane Austen) to create on small canvases.[3] The same anxiety of authorship, according to Gilbert and Gubar, compels women writers to construct a private, domestic world. In short, Stafford's proclivity toward the short story, and her interest in the quotidian world of women and children, result at least in part from her sex. Gilbert and Gubar argue, further, that the woman writer's anxiety of authorship influences her to look for a female role model. For American women authors of Stafford's generation, these models were invariably writers of the short story: Edith Wharton, Katherine Anne Porter, Kay Boyle, Sarah Orne Jewett, Kate Chopin, Willa Cather.

Whatever the reasons that Jean Stafford wrote such successful short stories, she presented her attitudes about the ironic dilemmas of modern human beings largely by means of women. As in the novels, in her short stories Stafford creates a variety of feminine situations. From a five-year-old girl whose father, in a rage against her mother, cuts her treasured golden curls, robbing her not only of her favored status in the family but of her identity, to a bedridden old woman who has lost all speech except nouns and pronouns and whose sole diversions are food and a nasty parrot, Stafford's short stories present the concerns and problems of females at virtually every age.

Curiously, no critic has analyzed Stafford's canon from a feminist perspective, or even noted that most of her characters are women and most of her situations "feminine"; yet throughout her work she exhibits an enlightened awareness of the position of women in a patriarchal society.[4] As in *The Catherine Wheel*, in her stories Stafford confronts the dilemma that occurs when women's attempts to create and maintain their own identities, and their refusal to change or inability to compromise their own selfhood by subjugating themselves to others, result in an extreme and ultimately unacceptable isolation,

3. Gilbert and Gubar, *Madwoman in the Attic*, Chap. 2.
4. In her recent book *Jean Stafford* (Boston, 1985), Mary Ellen Williams Walsh recognizes Stafford's interest in female characters and situations, but her critical approach is not feminist.

a withdrawal from human interaction. As always, Stafford's modernist, ironic vision allows no clear-cut, unequivocal perspective; in her
stories, her contemporary, feminist attitudes are undercut by her traditional, conservative impulses. And the interaction and juxtaposition of these disparate visions result in a complex, ambiguous fictional world.

Among the most memorable of Jean Stafford's characters are her
elderly women, and typical of her old, usually bitter women is eighty-
two-year-old Rhoda Bellamy, spinster and protagonist of "The Hope
Chest." She lies in bed on a gray Christmas morning remembering
the fiasco of her Boston debut over a half century before—"a mis-
carriage so sensational" that she and her parents fled to Maine, where
after her mother's early death, "she and her father dwelt together in
angry disappointment" (*CS*, 113). Miss Bellamy recalls too the small
boy who bravely appeared at her front door the day before, peddling
a spruce wreath. Although her original intention was to rebuff the
boy ("I will eat you, little boy," she thinks, "because once upon a time
I, too, had pink cheeks and a fair skin and clear eyes. And don't you
deny it"), their haggling over the price of the wreath culminates in
her agreement to pay the requested twenty-five cents in exchange for
a kiss (*CS*, 114).

Alone and querulous, Rhoda Bellamy is at the end of a wasted life.
Her unwillingness to confront the world outside herself, as she "stead-
fastly [holds] her eyes closed, resisting the daylight," is apparently a
lifelong malady, for "she had been like that as a child, she had loved
sleep better than eating or playing" (*CS*, 114). Willfully naïve, she
avoids reality, wondering, for example, whether the noise outside her
house is that of a destructive dog "defiling my lawn and littering the
garden with things I do not like to know exist." She distrusts her
fellowman; Rhoda Bellamy is a woman who "pride[s] herself on never
having been tricked by anyone" (*CS*, 115). Her Christmas wish is that
her attentive maid will "come before I die of loneliness," and as the
story ends the empty old woman, denied even the solace of normal
grief, "nurse[s] her hurt like a baby at a milkless breast, with tear-
less eyes" (*CS*, 117, 119).

Mrs. Chester Ramsey, like Rhoda Bellamy and Lucy Pride aged

and aristocratic, consciously resists awareness and adaptation in "The Captain's Gift." "I have never liked change," she tells the friends and relatives who encourage her to leave her run-down neighborhood, "and now I am too old for it" (*CS*, 439). She remains in her New York townhouse, and "the ivory tower in which she lives is impregnable to the ill-smelling, rude-sounding, squalid-looking world which through the years has moved in closer and closer and now surrounds her on all sides. Incredibly, she has not been swallowed up" (*CS*, 439). Although nostalgic for the days, long ago, when the area was aristocratic and she was well-known, Mrs. Ramsey neither dislikes her altered neighborhood nor resents "that none of them knows that she alone belongs here," for she is oblivious of her immediate environment and of the larger world as well (*CS*, 439). It is wartime, but the old woman is completely ignorant of the world situation. Although the numerous well-bred young men of her acquaintance are in uniform and overseas, she writes to them as though they are carefree youths on a holiday, and "mothers of the soldiers are overjoyed; she is their link with the courtly past, she is Mrs. Wharton at first hand" (*CS*, 441, 442).

On the afternoon on which the story occurs, Mrs. Ramsey welcomes a parcel from her favorite grandson, who habitually sends his grandmother elegant trinkets from Europe. Although the young man's mother, her daughter, has commented that in his letters the boy is "becoming more and more unrecognizable," Mrs. Ramsey is unprepared for his latest gift, a thick braid of blond hair that she pushes, in revulsion, to the floor, where it lies "shining like a living snake" (*CS*, 444, 445). The braid, with its connotations of mortality, stuns the old woman, and as the story ends, "She speaks aloud in the empty room. 'How unfriendly, Arthur!' she says. 'How unkind!' And as if there were a voice in the hair at her feet, she distinctly heard him saying, 'There's a war on, hadn't you heard?'" (*CS*, 445).

Clearly Mrs. Ramsey, the "innocent child of seventy-five," is an alien in a war-torn modern world. Oblivious of reality, she must, as the ending of the story demonstrates, be awakened. And yet, because she is "a visitor from a distant time," she is—for Jean Stafford and for the reader—sympathetic and attractive (*CS*, 442). She is an Edwardian lady with an "expansive feminine elegance," and the reader, as well as the narrator, regrets that her revelation is inevitable: "Since there are so few years left to her (and since there is now no danger of our being bombed) it would be unkind and playful sacrilege to destroy her illusion that the world is still good and beautiful and harmonious in all its parts. She need never know how barbarically civilization has been betrayed" (*CS*, 440, 441). But Mrs. Ramsey must be awakened, however belatedly, to the verities of life. Jean Stafford knows that however seductive the cocoon of isolation, adulthood necessitates interaction with other human beings, which often brings disillusionment.

Mrs. Ramsey and Rhoda Bellamy can ignore the world in part because they can afford to; Isobel Carpenter would maintain that she cannot afford not to. Although the protagonist of "Life Is No Abyss" is twenty-year-old orphaned Lily Carpenter, Isobel, sixty years her senior, is the memorable character in the story. After investment broker Cousin Will, Lily's guardian, loses Isobel's money, she refuses offers to live with him or other cousins, and takes up residence in the poorhouse. "Loving every minute of her hardship," she reigns happily as "self-appointed" family martyr and victim (*CS*, 93). Isobel's pitiable life-style is, like the other elderly female characters', the result of her inability to adapt. When Will's lack of business sense renders her penniless ("her descent to threadbare penury had been lightning-paced, so fast that it had had in itself a kind of theatrical splendor"), Isobel is "not equipped to modify her way of life at all: she could not and she would not substitute, she could only and she would only lose" (*CS*, 99).

For Lily, whose first visit to the dreary, malodorous institution is a frightening lesson in poverty and old age, her fractious cousin's cruelty to Will and the rest of the family is unforgivable. Her epiphany occurs as she watches Viola, Isobel's blind roommate, mindlessly sing.

> The generic face had seemed to be no more than a clever armature to support the promontories, apertures and embellishments because neither knowledge nor experience was written on it; its only signature was that of absolute and monstrous poverty. It was a parody, the scaffolding of ageless bone; it was an illustration, a paradigm of total, lifelong want. Because there had been no progress in the life . . . there could be no retrogression, so that this woman could not say—if, indeed, she could speak at all—as Cousin Isobel could, "Once I was that and now I am this. Once I dwelt in marble halls and now I live in quarters that the least of my serfs have scorned," and take from the contrast a certain satisfaction, galling as it might be. To descend, however ignobly, was,

nevertheless, to participate. In speaking of Cousin Isobel's tribulations, it was possible to use verbs: she had lost her money, she had been ruined, she had plunged from the highest heights to the lowest depths. But to the woman who had been born without the most important sense and, as Cousin Isobel had implied, been born witless, only adjectives were applicable: she was blind, alone, animal. (*CS*, 104–105).

Isobel perceives Viola as "the embodiment of what Will Hamilton has brought me to," but to Lily, Viola's emptiness is her "state of grace," her salvation. For Lily, Viola's song is the blind woman's assurance that life is no abyss. Perplexed by her paradoxical recognition that only Viola, who can neither give nor take, truly loves, Lily rejects Isobel, whose obstinate choice not to live fully, not to love, is inconceivable (*CS*, 110, 112).

Impoverished Isobel is an unusual character in Stafford's canon, for despite the significance of poverty and wealth in several of her stories, economics is not often a consideration in her work. Her characters are usually too young or too old—or too female—to be directly concerned with financial matters, or as in the case of Lucy Pride, Katharine Congreve, and others, too rich. Or, as women, they are traditionally prevented from having control of money. Stafford's setting of her stories so frequently on Sundays and holidays further subordinates the concern with money.

With her elderly women Stafford explores the tragedy of a failure to participate in life. These characters are, by virtue of their age, removed from the everyday world and its exigencies. Withdrawn from sexual entanglements and the vicissitudes of life, they can ignore societal expectations. Stafford's younger female heroes, however, are necessarily more vulnerable to society and its attitudes about women, and more accountable for their reactions to the difficulties of modern life. In "The End of a Career," Stafford examines the tragic and absurd lengths to which women can go to resist age and rejection. Angelica Early, a beauty from birth, achieves international fame and acclaim for her remarkable good looks. Married to an older man who spends his time hunting in exotic locales, lonely Angelica's avocation is the adornment of "yachts and chateaux and boxes at the opera" of "extremely rich people" around the world (*CS*, 449). She dedicates herself to the preservation of her beauty with conventual discipline and eschews the complications of life: "Apart from her beauty, there was not a good deal to be said about Angelica." She has money, but not enough to make her very rich; style and charm, but without the flair of the eccentric or the avant-garde. She doesn't flirt, dazzle, or cause trouble: "She was simply and solely a beautiful woman" (*CS*, 449).

Angelica's dedication to the cultivation of her gift demands daily attention to massages, dyes, and makeup, and as she enters her forties, an annual retreat to a sanitarium in Normandy, where her skin, the outer layer being flayed, is restored to its youthful vigor by the steel-wire brush of an odious doctor. She returns from these mysterious sojourns so invigorated that her acquaintances are convinced that she has a secret lover. They do not know that Angelica has sacrificed her very life for their adoration, that she is without friends and family, that in her consecration to her beauty

> she had been obliged to pass up much of the miscellany of life that irritates but also brings about the evolution of personality; the unmolested oyster creates no pearl. Her heart might be shivered, she might be inwardly scorched with desire or mangled with jealousy and greed, she might be be-numbed by loneliness and doubt, but she was so unswerving in her trusteeship of her perfection that she could not allow anxiety to pleat her immaculate brow or anger to discolor her damask cheeks or tears to deflower her eyes. Perhaps, like an artist, she was not always grateful for this talent of beauty that destiny had imposed upon her without asking leave, but, like the artist, she knew where her duty lay.
>
> (*CS*, 450–51)

Eventually Angelica's age begins to tell on her hands, which the doctor cannot rejuvenate. "Go and find a lover," he advises his distraught patient. "To be loved is to be beautiful, but to be beautiful is not necessarily to be loved" (*CS*, 456). But for Angelica, the advice comes too late, and "now . . . unbearably sad that she had been obliged to tread a straight-and-narrow path with not a primrose on it, [she] would sigh and nearly cry and say, 'What have I done with my life?'" (*CS*, 455). Devastated by the inexorable assault of age, Angelica takes to her bed—and, like other Stafford characters who try to avoid involvement in the world, begins to sleep throughout the day— a move that her "friends" attribute first to the end of the imagined love affair, later to illness: "They . . . would never have dreamed it was despair that she groped through sightlessly, in a vacuum everlasting and black" (*CS*, 460). When her only relative, an aunt, arrives from the West and elicits the truth from her niece too late, only hours before Angelica dies of despair, she comments that the beauty's is "unquestionably the saddest [story] she had ever heard" (*CS*, 462).

A good, simple woman, "the least predatory of women," Angelica is preyed upon and destroyed by the people who claim to care about her (*CS*, 449). She is a "masterpiece," an "ornament," an art object allowed only to adorn, not to live as she would like (*CS*, 450, 449). Angelica's tale is a comment on the superficiality of modern society, the selfishness and insensitivity of human beings, and the tragedy of those whose reluctance to risk hurt and change denies them a normal life; hers is the tragedy of a person denied all but a surface self. And yet, despite the universality of "The End of a Career," it presents a distinctly female situation. Men generally cannot be destroyed by the loss of their looks, because they are not usually so valued for them. For women in a patriarchal society and of a certain age, time is a particularly perilous enemy.

At fifty, Angelica Early, like Mrs. Ramsey and, to some extent, Katharine Congreve, is an anomalous innocent. Plagued throughout her life by her extraordinary beauty, she simply does not recognize— until it is too late—that her life is void of meaning. She is genuinely surprised and perplexed by her doctor's failure to stay the process of age and his counsel that she should find solace in love. "Were not these the things she should have been told when she was a girl growing up? Why had no one, in this long life of hers, which had been peopled by such a multitude, warned her to lay up a store of good things against the famine of old age?" (*CS*, 457). Angelica's naïveté, like Mrs. Ramsey's, is her immunity from the responsibility for her death; but in the first-person narrator of "I Love Someone," Stafford creates a woman whose failure to engage life is conscious and, therefore, reproachable.

Upon her return from the funeral of a lifelong friend who has unexpectedly and inexplicably committed suicide, Jenny Peck muses that their common friends must feel that "it would have been better if, assuming that one of us had to take the overdose of sleeping pills, it had been I" (*CS*, 416–17). While Marigold Trask had been a beautiful, charming, apparently happy wife and mother, "I," Jenny thinks, "have never married and my death would discommode no one" (*CS*, 417). Although she believes that her friends care for her, "in a world unfit for solitary living," they cannot truly understand "the heart of a spinster which is at once impoverished and prodigal, at once unloving and lavishly soft" (*CS*, 417). They have, therefore, created their own image of their unmarried friend, who is, they believe, calm and unemotional. "I never make drastic changes in my life," Jenny corroborates. "I seldom rearrange my furniture; I have worn the same hairdress for twenty years" (*CS*, 417).

Like Angelica's friends, Jenny's imagine a youthful, tragic love affair, but the truth is that at forty-three Jenny Peck has never loved.

> There has been nothing in my life. I have lived the whole of it in the half-world of brief flirtations . . . of friendships that have perished of the cold or have hung on, desiccated, outliving their meaning and never once realizing the possibility of love. . . . From childhood I have unfailingly taken all the detours around passion and dedication; or say it this way, I have been a pilgrim without faith, traveling in an anticipation of loss, certain that the grail will have been spirited away by the time I have reached my journey's end. If I did not see in myself this skepticism, this unconditional refusal, this—I admit it—contempt, I would find it degrading that no one has ever proposed marriage to me. I do not wish to refuse but I do not know how to accept. In my ungivingness, I am more dead now, this evening, than Marigold Trask in her suburban cemetery.
>
> (*CS*, 418)

Jenny recognizes the seductions and advantages of her remoteness, knows that she, "dwelling upon the rim of life, see[s] everyone in the arena as acting blindly." She perceives that "far from the stage and safe, I, who never act on impulse, know nearly precisely the outcome of my always rational behavior. It makes me a woman without hope; but since there is no hope there is also no despair" (*CS*, 420). Like Katharine Congreve, rational Jenny cannot conceive of a loss of control over her life, but her subconscious mind—like Katharine's—thinks its own thoughts, and "sometimes I can feel the pain through the anesthetic," she admits (*CS*, 418). Her final perception, at the story's end, reaffirms Stafford's belief that real life is worth the risks: "My friends and I have managed my life with the best of taste and all that is lacking at this banquet where the appointments are so elegant is something to eat" (*CS*, 422).

Because she is more aware, Jenny is more culpable than Angelica Early; indeed, there is no evidence that the emptiness of her life is anyone's fault but her own. Yet it is significant in the story and in her life that Jenny suffers from the "incurable but unblemishing disease" of spinsterhood (*CS*, 419). For Polly Bay there is still time. A German teacher at Nevilles College, Polly is the only Bay family member of her generation to remain in Adams, Colorado (Stafford's fictional name for Boulder, where she grew up). She lives in the oppressive ancestral home of her aged aunt and uncle, whose primary interests are reminiscing about their dead forebears and castigating their descendants who have abandoned Colorado for the depraved East, which they hate with a vehemence that belies the fact that they have never been east of the Mississippi River. If not particularly happy with her life, Polly "had not been inspired to escape" until five months earlier, when, on a Christmas visit to her sister in Boston, she had met Robert Fair. He is a divorced professor whose proposal of marriage "had seemed to release in her an inexhaustible wellspring of life; until that moment she had not known that she was dying, that she was being killed—by inches, but surely killed—by her aunt and uncle and by the green yearlings in her German class and by the dogmatic monotony of the town's provincialism" (*CS*, 318).

Polly knows now, exhibiting the pervasive female fear of enclosure that reflects woman's "sense of powerlessness, her fear that she inhabits strange and incomprehensible places," that she is being strangled in her ancestral home, in which the large rooms are so overfurnished that "you had no sense of space in them and, on the contrary, felt cornered and nudged and threatened by hanging lamps with dangerous dependencies and by the dark, bucolic pictures of Polly's forebears that leaned forward from the wall in their insculptured brassy frames" (*CS*, 308).[5] Now, as the spring semester ends, Polly must tell her intimidating aunt and uncle of her secret engagement and her intention to leave them. They by turns try to reason with their niece, argue with her, attempt to bribe her, appeal to her sense of duty, and "at no time did they accept the fact that she was going" (*CS*, 319). Polly, however, who recognizes finally, "appalled and miserably ashamed of herself, that she had never once insisted on her own identity in this house," feels invincible now that she has finally taken her stand, and when, just before her departure, her sister calls with the incredible news that Robert Fair has suddenly died, she hesitates only briefly

5. Gilbert and Gubar, *Madwoman in the Attic*, 84.

before deciding that she must go to Boston nonetheless. She boards
the train for the East with the recognition that though she has been
lonely, "I am not lonely now" (*CS*, 318, 310, 322).

A fairly straightforward account of a young person's struggle for
freedom from family and the past—with a characteristically Staffordian ironic twist on the traditional American journey from east to
west—"The Liberation" offers an intriguing variation on Stafford's
saga of women's lives. Polly is nearly thirty, and when her well-
meaning captors "compliment" her on having "reached 'a sensible
age' . . . it was a struggle for them not to use the word 'spinster.'"
Because Polly is thirty and single, "they had long ago stopped fearing
that she, too, might go" (*CS*, 306). They—and, for a time, Polly—
accept that only with the emotional and financial security of marriage
would she leave them. It is, of course, the prospect of marriage that
precipitates Polly's recognition of her discontent, and she seems to
feel genuine affection for her fiancé. When, at his death, her sister
encourages the momentarily reticent Polly to flee anyway, the question she poses in response—"Do you think that was why I was going
to marry him? Just to escape this house and this town?"—may elicit a
"yes" from the reader, but Polly believes otherwise (*CS*, 321). Earlier
in the story, however, "She could not remember of her fiancé anything
beyond his name, and, a little ruefully and a little cynically, she wondered if it was love of him or boredom with freshmen and with her
aunt and uncle that had caused her to get engaged to him" (*CS*, 307).
In "The Liberation," Stafford criticizes the mores of a society that can
envision for women only enslavement—to family, to the past, to marriage—and presents, in a female character who rejects society's restrictions, a human being who overcomes the temptations of stasis to
confront an unknown fate.

So Polly, it seems, may avoid the "incurable disease" of spinsterhood, but among the more wretched and pitiful of her fellow female
characters are those not so fortunate. Jean Stafford's short stories
are populated with stereotypical old maids and stereotypical attitudes toward them. Rose Fabrizio, the young protagonist of "The
Bleeding Heart," assumes that the anonymous invalid next door,
whose "venomous and senile whimper" so annoys her, is a "peaked
spinster" (*CS*, 155). She is, Rose learns later, the mother of the man
she fancies as her adopted father. Marie's aunt, in Stafford's first

story, "And Lots of Solid Color," is a "dried old spinster" who exults in her niece's failure to find a job. About her, Stafford writes, "There was nothing left in that old body, nothing beautiful in the old mind, nothing ugly either, just something that was old and crippled and pathetic." Fräulein Schmetzer, the landlady in "The Cavalier," is a fat, woeful, "panicky spinster," who is, "by her own confession, the wretchedest woman alive, because she had never married and never had children," and whose "wasted womanhood" is demonstrated in her feeble attempts to mother Duane, the protagonist, and in her fascination with the lurid misfortunes of her relatives.[6]

Jean Stafford offers a different perspective on the trials of single women in her portraits of divorcees. These women, who are rarely major characters in Stafford's work, hover in the background of a number of her stories, providing comedy, like Mrs. Fowler in "Beatrice Trueblood's Story," who "hated men so passionately that no one could dream why she married so many of them"; or pathos, like the women in "A Modest Proposal" who flock to the Caribbean for "their six weeks' quarantine" that will cure them of marriage, and who are "spoken of as invalids; they were said to be here for 'the cure.' Some of them did look ill and shocked as if, at times, they could not remember why they had come" (CS, 388, 66). These women, and the widows with whom they share a new independence from men, do not permanently reject a fulfilling life. They are recent "orphans" for whom the end of a marriage often spells at least a temporary withdrawal, "that group who have spent their lives leaning on someone—or being leaned on by—a father, a mother, a husband; and who, when the casket is closed or the divorce decree is final, find that they are waifs" (CS, 22).

Abby Reynolds, in "The Children's Game," has joined the ranks of these "forlorn, brave orphans," having moved, in the year since her husband's death, "from a Florentine *pensione* for bereft or virginal gentlewomen to the same kind of asylum in Rome" (CS, 21). Now Abby has begun to feel "quaint and wan" and "indistinguishable from the thousands and thousands of lonesome American ladies who lived abroad because a foreign address, however modest, had a cachet that a New York or a Boston apartment hotel had not; the cachet was necessary so that they would not be pitied" (CS, 21–22). Recognizing at

6. Jean Stafford, "And Lots of Solid Color," *American Prefaces*, V (1939), 23, and "The Cavalier," *New Yorker*, February 12, 1949, p. 31.

last that "she despised the flaccid life she was living and that she
wanted to be back in the thick of things, among her innumerable energetic friends, in the familiar and surprising streets of New York,"
Abby books passage for two weeks later and spends the intervening
time with Hugh Nicholson, an old friend of hers and her husband's
(*CS*, 23). Her emotional rebirth is hastened by the attentions of a
man, and "Abby realized that it was the removal from her life of
John's energy that had enervated her, and energy was what she admired and, moreover, required as dearly as food and drink and air.
She could burn, that is, with her own flame, but she must be re-
kindled; she must be complemented so that she could maintain her
poise and pride. She was not the sort of woman who could live alone
satisfactorily" (*CS*, 25). Finding herself falling in love with Hugh,
Abby nonetheless rejects the prospect of a long-term relationship
with him, not so much, it seems, because of his estranged wife, but
because his "remoteness [is] constitutional" (*CS*, 28). Nonetheless,
"Hugh was the agent that reminded her that she must seek a husband" (*CS*, 26).

"The Children's Game," like *The Catherine Wheel*, and "The Liberation" and other stories, clearly manifests Jean Stafford's complex and
ambiguous attitudes about female behavior in our society. Abby's retreat from active life is precipitated by the loss of a man, and her return (which is facilitated by another man) apparently necessitates the
acquisition of yet another. Stafford's message? To live at all, a woman
must live with—and for—a man. And yet, as always, the situation
is more complex. Although Hugh Nicholson's attentions renew the
widow and help her to "redeem her spirit, that had so long been mis-
laid," her decision to abandon her "negative life" in Europe predates
Hugh's appearance (*CS*, 25, 26). And although weak, forlorn Hugh,
addicted to gambling and rejected by his wife, would like a future
with Abby, she, like Katharine Congreve, decides that she cannot
sacrifice herself to his salvation: "She would not have given up so
easily; she would have died hard; would, out of vanity and love, said
that she could, somehow, save him; she would have staked everything
on him if she had not so fully understood him" (*CS*, 33). Again,
Stafford presents a protagonist who accepts the traditional belief that
women are defined and made whole by men but whose actions demonstrate her strength and autonomy.

Since women in Stafford's world are so often perceived by them-selves and others in terms of their relationships with men, and since the fate of unmarried women in her work is usually bleak, it seems inevitable that marriage is for her the preferred life-style. But An-gelica Early's sham marriage and Marigold Trask's suicide demon-strate that for Stafford marriage is not a panacea. In fact, happy marriages are rare in her fiction. Emily Vanderpool's parents are ap-parently compatible in the comic stories "Bad Characters," "A Read-ing Problem," "The Violet Rock," and "The Scarlet Letter," but adults are insignificant in these stories. The Heaths appear to coexist amicably enough in "Polite Conversation," yet one wonders how Mar-garet, captive in the social ritual of afternoon tea with her garrulous neighbors, really feels about her eccentric husband's refusal to join her. A rare male point-of-view character, Evan Leckie, in "The Maid-en," bitter about his wife's abandonment of him, becomes entranced with Frau Reinmuth's "ineffable femininity" and envies her seemingly perfect marriage (*CS*, 57). His discovery that the young Herr Rein-muth proposed marriage in the euphoria inspired by his attendance at an execution by guillotine (the maiden of the story), however, de-stroys the aura of romance and undermines the couple's happiness in Evan's eyes.

Far more typical in Stafford's fictional world are marriages like that of five-year-old Hannah's parents in "Cops and Robbers." Hannah, the protagonist of the story, is the innocent pawn in the bitter fight between her bibulous, increasingly contentious parents. Her father becomes jealous when Hannah and her mother, with their identical blond hair, sit for a portrait that is to displace a paternal heirloom in the drawing room and, in a misplaced attack on his wife, has his daughter's luxurious curls shorn. Her mother is as devastated as Hannah. "I cannot believe that criminals are any more ingenious than wives and husbands when their marriages are turning sour," she pro-nounces (*CS*, 432). In her other numerous short stories that deal principally with marriage, Stafford—herself thrice married and twice divorced—is no less critical in her presentation.

"The Connoisseurs" are Mary and Donald Rand, two young, pro-fessional travelers who, when they continually run into each other throughout Europe, decide that they are fated to be together. They marry and, for two years, travel happily together. But while Donald is, it appears, inherently peripatetic, Mary wanders the globe with a goal; she seeks "the Place where the status quo would have a meaning beyond mere contentment." When the war retires the couple to a sedentary life at home in New York, they discover that they have nothing in common and that they dislike each other. Without constantly shifting settings, "they could not lose themselves and therefore could not find each other." The end of the war revalidates their passports, and the petulant pair resume their wandering in an effort to rekindle their love. But the exertion, as Mary recognizes, is futile: "Travel, to Mary Rand, had come to be the name of a neurosis, and it was on travel that she blamed the hurricanes that rocked her marriage and seemed at last to have wrecked it. It had been travel that had brought them together in the first place; travel, she thought bitterly, and absolutely nothing else." When she realizes later that she and Donald are doomed to remain together, to be miserable, never to find the magic place, she sees "the rest of her life stretching out before her like a flat western prairie without a single altitude to vary the monotony." [7]

In "The Connoisseurs" Stafford again betrays her somewhat adulterated acceptance of the traditional myths about women. Mary, in her longing for "some cranny of the earth where happiness, already made, awaited," exhibits the nesting instinct, the desire for domesticity, that is widely accepted as a female characteristic. And she believes that a man, not she herself, will find the special place. Even before she meets Donald she is "affianced in her imagination to the man who would discover for her that perfect place; she thought of herself not as an aimless traveler but as a pilgrim with a goal. She felt certain that when, with her guide, she entered Eden, she would be content to let her passport molder and her trunk keys rust." More significantly, Mary resists the possibility of a divorce, even before her ultimate recognition that she and Donald must remain in guilt and misery together: "Although he maddened her, although she sometimes questioned that she loved him and although she was certain that nothing short of a miracle could bring about the restitution of their concord, the thought of parting stunned her." [8] Apparently, mar-

7. Jean Stafford, "The Connoisseurs," *Harper's Bazaar*, LXXXVI (October, 1952), 239, 240, 232, 240.
8. *Ibid.*, 232.

riage does not guarantee that a woman will avoid the inertia that plagues so many of Stafford's single women; indeed, it often exacerbates her reluctance to accept change.

In "An Influx of Poets," for example, Stafford's autobiographical hero Cora Savage Maybank, though she fantasizes about her insensitive husband's death and even imagines her second marriage, cannot really conceive of leaving him. The story is one of two that Stafford's editor, Robert Giroux, extracted after her death from her unfinished novel, *The Parliament of Women*. Its interest lies not only in its considerable literary merit but in the fact that it apparently faithfully represents Stafford's view of her marriage to the poet Robert Lowell. Narrated by Cora, "An Influx of Poets" begins in "that awful summer . . . the first summer after the war [when] every poet in America came to stay with us" and gradually fills in the history of her five-year marriage to the young Bostonian poet Theron Maybank. Cora writes of Theron's enthusiastic embrace of Catholicism and her heretical doubts, and of the tension evoked by the conflict between his insistence that they embrace a life of total poverty and her desire for, and ultimate attainment of, "what I had striven for from the beginning: a house and a lawn and trees." The pious poet scorns his wife's nesting instinct as "plebeian, anti-intellectual, lace-curtain Irish." Cora comments, "God almighty! Never was a man so set on knocking the stuffing out of his bride!" Eventually she wonders, "What had become of the joking lad I'd married?"[9]

Since Cora, a high-school English teacher, supports the couple, they move to the cherished house in Maine and prepare for the annual summer influx of poets. But the genuine solaces of her own home and the false consolations of alcohol cannot assuage her intensifying dissatisfaction with her abusive, contentious husband. She suffers from constant headaches and resists telling Theron, who, she knows, "whether he crowed or shrugged . . . would undermine me . . . would cripple me and make me mute." When the local doctor suggests that the headaches may be psychological in origin, Cora is torn between her conviction that her illness is physiological and the enticing prospect of using her illness to escape her husband. "After accepting Dr. Lowebridge's diagnosis," she conjectures, "Theron was almost bound to send me to New York lest the news that I was 'mental' be

9. Jean Stafford, "An Influx of Poets," *New Yorker*, November 6, 1978, pp. 43, 55, 51, 49.

noised about in Boston and such a separation, justified and temporary, was what I had prayed for all these stewed and sleeplessly stew-
ing nights of summer." Cora intersperses her "wifely duties" (caring
for their houseguests and typing Theron's poems) with daydreams
that free her from "the barbed-wire fences (some of them electric) of
my marriage," and wonders "what my life would have been if I had
married someone else, or what it still could be if Theron drowned." [10]

With the arrival of Minnie Rosoff, the recently divorced wife of one
of the "baby bards," who is clearly attracted to Theron, Cora constructs a new scenario, imagining now that the two drown together,
and that "honorably widowed, I was free. Or they fell in love and their
adultery exonerated me of all my capital crimes and all my pec-
cadilloes and all my hyprocrisies and self-indulgences. . . . Dishon-
ored, I would ascend refreshed, putting aside the ruin of this marriage shattered so ignominiously by *the other woman*, by that most
unseemly of disgraces, above all by something *not my fault*, giving
me the uncontested right to hate him. And I would come eventually
into a second marriage: I saw my husband and I saw my sons." Later,
however, Cora regrets her fantasy. Echoing Katharine Congreve,
she warns the reader, "Be careful what you wish for, be wary of the
predicates of your fantasies and lies." Imagining that Theron and
Minnie would fall in love, she never believed that it could happen, that
she "*would* taste the vilest degradation, the bitterest jealousy, the
most scalding and vindictive rancor." [11] But the seemingly impossible
occurs, and Theron and Cora close up the house and travel to Boston,
where they part, Cora headed for New York and an appointment with
a psychoanalyst.

Stafford's final short story is one of the most blatant manifesta-
tions of her inheritance of the female literary tradition. Herein, for
example, the female desire for domesticity that is implicit in *The
Catherine Wheel* and stories like "And Lots of Solid Color"—as well
as, apparently, in Stafford's own life—becomes a central theme, calling to mind the traditionally feminine representations of "female
space" that Gilbert and Gubar have documented in *The Madwoman
in the Attic*. [12] Relegated to, in some sense imprisoned in, their homes,
women demonstrate in their writing the fact that they are stifled,

10. *Ibid.*, 44, 43.
11. *Ibid.*, 55, 55–56.
12. Gilbert and Gubar, Chaps. 2, 3.

trapped, buried in interior spaces, as well as the dark mythic knowledge of the cave that they, because they inhabit and are familiar with such womblike places, can comprehend more thoroughly than men. When Cora, noting that "all my life I had been making houses for myself," delights in "*my* house (my very own, my first and very own)," she articulates the affinity for domestic enclosures that women writers have long recreated in their female characters; when she speaks of the "barbed-wire fences" of her marriage, she articulates the fear of entrapment that is the other side of the mirror.[13]

Stafford's manipulation of the facts of the demise of her relationship with Robert Lowell discloses some of her attitudes about male-female relationships. In "An Influx of Poets," Cora has no literary ambitions and seems relatively content to subjugate herself to her husband's talent. Actually, Stafford, though she was at the time a more successful author than her husband, regularly (as Eileen Simpson recalls in *Poets in Their Youth*) interrupted her writing in order to type Lowell's poems and feed their guests. While Stafford resented some intrusions into her work, such as teaching, Simpson observes that "the typing chores Jean seemed to accept as a wifely duty." Further, in the story, Cora inherits from an aunt the money that enables her to buy the house in Maine; whereas in reality the house that Stafford and Lowell bought in Damariscotta Mills was paid for by the profits from *Boston Adventure*.[14] Stafford's sensitivity to her literary and economic success (and Robert Lowell's lack of it) made her unable to admit, in fiction, that she earned the money for a house.

Cora Maybank's mental illness, which was apparently biographically accurate, since soon after her separation from Lowell in September, 1946, Jean Stafford was admitted to Payne Whitney Clinic in New York for a "psycho-alcoholic cure," echoes the reaction to the trials of marriage and the modern world of a number of Stafford's female protagonists. Stafford's fascination with madness and the seductive attractions of the "interior castle," which she introduced in *Boston Adventure*, in turn echoes the preoccupation of many women writers with mental illness. Theorists and literary critics have long recognized the connections between women's expectations and alter-

13. Stafford, "An Influx of Poets," 43.
14. Eileen Simpson, *Poets in Their Youth: A Memoir* (New York, 1982), 123, 134, 116.

natives in a male culture and the ubiquity of mental illness among women. The woman writer's anxiety of authorship, her awareness that she is the "other" in a male environment, manifests itself, as Gilbert and Gubar and others have maintained, in a "dis-ease or, at any rate, a disaffection, a disturbance, a distrust, that spreads like a stain throughout the style and structure of much literature by women."[15]

Women writers often reserve their most trenchant portraits of female madness for wives. "In fiction describing the mad wife," Pratt writes, "women authors create their most complex embellishments on the enclosure archetype." Young women, single women, and old women are aware of the stereotypes and restrictions that surround their status, but married women often, it seems, entertain naïve ideas about their worth and independence. "Freedom to come and go, which involves the right to make decisions about one's own time, work, and other activities, is a basic element of authenticity. The irony that permeates so much of women's fiction results from a recognition of the discrepancy between premarital dreams of authenticity and marital realities."[16] The intelligent, mature woman for whom marriage is a trap often withdraws into herself from the recognition that she is being stifled by a freely chosen, ostensibly happy lifestyle. For Stafford, the withdrawal from the horrors of modern society—and, for women, from the oppressions of a patriarchal culture—is a powerful temptation; her fiction demonstrates that the most dangerous and enticing of avoidance techniques is the retreat to one's own mind.

In one of her best-known and most successful short stories, "A Country Love Story," Stafford intensifies her exploration of marriage and the solaces and dangers of the withdrawal within. Thirty-year-old May, married to a history professor some twenty years her senior, moves with her husband to the country so that he can continue his convalescence from a long illness. Although May believes that a return to university life will hasten Daniel's recovery (and she herself longs for the resumption of their active life), his doctor recommends the retreat to the country. When May protests, the doctor's portentous rejoinder settles the question: "You are bound to find him

15. Hamilton, *Robert Lowell*, 119; Gilbert and Gubar, *Madwoman in the Attic*, 51.
16. Pratt, *Archetypal Patterns in Women's Fiction*, 51, 45.

changed a little. A long illness removes a thoughtful man from his fellow beings. It is like living with an exacting mistress who is not content with half a man's attention but must claim it all" (*CS*, 135). Rural life is pleasant for awhile, as urbanites May and Daniel explore the countryside and renovate their first house. But as the summer and its pastimes end and Daniel resumes his scholarly work, May grows bored. Without occupation, she begins to long for her busy life in Boston, and escapes from her desires and the guilt that they inspire by sleeping for hours throughout the day. The sleep—into which Cora Maybank, calling it "the most delectable condition on earth," escapes too—is a defense against May's guilt over her discontent: "Longing, she was remorseful, as if by desiring another she betrayed this life, and, remorseful, she hid away in sleep" (*CS*, 137). But sleep can be only a temporary escape, and she and Daniel begin to quarrel; finally he suggests that they "just leave each other alone" (*CS*, 137).

Daniel becomes increasingly eccentric, and sensing May's unhappiness, he lashes out, accusing her of withholding something from him, and finally, of going mad. Ignored and then attacked by her husband, May comes to feel that "love, the very center of their being, was choked off, overgrown, invisible," and recognizes, quite suddenly, that "to the thin, ill scholar whose scholarship and illness had usurped her place, she had taken a weighty but unviolent dislike" (*CS*, 138). Now, as "she felt the cold old house somehow enveloping her as if it were their common enemy," even her cherished home changes from solace to trap (*CS*, 138). Lacking the love and attention of her husband, her friends and social diversions, and even a comfortable sense of place, she withdraws from the depressing world around her: "May now realized that she had no wish for the spring to come, no wish to plant a garden, and, branching out at random, she found she had no wish to see the sea again, or children, or favorite pictures, or even her own face on a happy day. For a minute or two, she was almost enraptured in this state of no desire, but then, purged swiftly of her cynicism, she knew it to be false, knew that actually she did have a desire—the desire for a desire" (*CS*, 139). As always, Stafford captures both the seductiveness and the danger of the retreat from the outer world. Accused of going mad, May, seeking revenge on Daniel, begins—like Cora Maybank—to imagine another life-style. Gazing out the kitchen window at the anachronistic antique sleigh that graces the yard, she envisions a lover.

> She might be a widow, she might be divorced, she might be committing
> adultery. Certainly there was no need to specify in an affair so securely
> legal. There was no need, that is, up to a point, and then the point came
> when she took in the fact that she not only believed in this lover but
> loved him and depended wholly on his companionship. She complained
> to him of Daniel and he consoled her; she told him stories of her girl-
> hood, when she had gaily gone to parties, squired by boys of her own
> age; she dazzled him sometimes with the wise comments she made on
> the books she read. It came to be true that if she so much as looked at
> the sleigh, she was weakened, failing with starvation. (*CS*, 141)

As she and her Casaubon-like husband grow further apart, May
becomes more and more obsessed with "the sleigh . . . and . . . the
man, her lover, who was connected with it somehow." She longs to but
cannot confess her aberrations to Daniel: "She was so separated from
the world, so far removed from his touch and his voice, so solitary,
that she would have sued a stranger for companionship" (*CS*, 143).
When, months later, in the spring, she suddenly sees her lover quite
clearly, sitting in the sleigh, she believes that Daniel is right, that she
is "bedeviled." But just as suddenly Daniel, awakening from his own
obsessions, cries, "The winter is over, May. You must forgive the hal-
lucinations of a sick man," and pleads, "If I am ever sick again, don't
leave me, May" (*CS*, 144). Now when May looks at the sleigh, "no one
was in it; nor had anyone been in it for many years." As the story
ends, a cat climbs into it "as if by careful plan," and "she knew now
that no change would come, and that she would never see her lover
again. Confounded utterly, like an orphan in solitary confinement, she
went outdoors and got into the sleigh. The blacksmith's imperturb-
able cat stretched and rearranged his position, and May sat beside
him with her hands locked tightly in her lap, rapidly wondering over
and over again how she would live the rest of her life" (*CS*, 145). May
returns, albeit reluctantly, to her traditional role as housewife and
helpmeet. Sitting, in the final image of the story, with her "hands
locked tightly in her lap," she is an obedient, subservient, anxious
wife. But she is not mad, not repudiating reality, and again Stafford
implies that woman's life of compromise is preferable to the false freedom of madness.

Pansy Vanneman recognizes that she must function in the world,
too, even though she has no husband to force her to confront reality. Stafford's most trenchant exploration of the retreat to the interior
castle of the mind is one of her most successful stories, "The Inte-

rior Castle." Pansy Vanneman, twenty-five, hospitalized in a strange city for serious head injuries sustained in an automobile accident, gazes out her hospital window at the unvarying view. The sky and the trees "seemed zealously determined to maintain a status quo," and like the landscape, Pansy, without visitors or diversions, is quiescent: "So perfect and stubborn was her body's immobility that it was as if the room and the landscape, mortified by the ice, were extensions of herself . . . the nurses said . . . that she might as *well* be dead for all the interest she took in life" (*CS*, 180, 181).

Pansy enjoys the nurses' perplexity, and "the more they courted her with offers of magazines, crossword puzzles, and a radio that she could rent from the hospital, the more she retired from them into herself and into the world which she had created in her long hours here and which no one could ever penetrate nor imagine" (*CS*, 182). Pansy's world recreates the traditional female writer's cavern of her mind, where she finds "the scattered leaves not only of her own power but of the tradition which might have generated that power. The body of her precursor's art, and thus the body of her own art, lies in pieces around her, dismembered, dis-remembered, disintegrated. How can she remember it and become a member of it, join it and rejoin it, integrate it and in doing so achieve her own integrity, her own selfhood?"[17] Pansy too cannot remember, or does not care to: "All she had been before and all the memories she might have brought out to disturb the monotony . . . were of no consequence to her. Not even in her thoughts did she employ more than a minimum of memory." Instead, she is entranced by her brain, her own dark cavern, "always pink and always fragile, always deeply interior and invaluable. She believed that she had reached the innermost chamber of knowledge and that perhaps her knowledge was the same as the saint's achievement of pure love. It was only convention, she thought, that made one say 'sacred heart' and not 'sacred brain'" (*CS*, 182–83).

But enemies from the world threaten Pansy's treasure. Pain and the doctor conspire to keep her from ultimate knowledge, and when, six weeks after the accident, the doctor begins to perform the "submucous resection" of her shattered nose, "in such pain as passed all language and even the farthest fetched analogies, she turned her eyes

17. Gilbert and Gubar, *Madwoman in the Attic*, 98.

inward, thinking that under the obscuring cloak of the surgeon's pain she could see her brain without the knowledge of its keeper" (*CS*, 189). But the doctor's torture is too severe, and "she was claimed entirely by this present meaningless pain and suddenly and sharply she forgot what she had meant to do. She was aware of nothing but her ascent to the summit of something; what it was she did not know, whether it was a tower or a peak or Jacob's ladder. Now she was an abstract word, now she was a theorem of geometry, now she was a kite flying, a prism flashing, a kaleidoscope turning" (*CS*, 189).

Exploring unanesthetized regions, the doctor awakens new pain.

> It was as if a tangle of tiny nerves were being cut dexterously, one by one; the pain writhed spirally and came to her who was a pink bird and sat on the top of a cone. The pain was a pyramid made of a diamond; it was an intense light; it was the hottest fire, the coldest chill, the highest peak, the fastest force, the furthest reach, the newest time. It possessed nothing of her but its one infinitesimal scene: beyond the screen as thin as gossamer, the brain trembled for its life, hearing the knives hunting like wolves outside, sniffing and snapping. Mercy! Mercy! cried the scalped nerves. (*CS*, 192)

Finally the doctor announces that the worst is over, and Pansy, closing her eyes, "this time and this time alone" sees—with imagery that echoes the presentation of Sonie's withdrawal within, in *Boston Adventure*—"her brain lying in a shell-pink satin case. It was a pink pearl, no bigger than a needle's eye, but it was so beautiful and so pure that its smallness made no difference. Anyhow, as she watched, it grew. It grew larger and larger until it was an enormous bubble that contained the surgeon and the whole room within its rosy luster" (*CS*, 192). And like the woman writer, whose "trip into the cavern of her own mind, despite (or perhaps because of) its falls in darkness, its stumblings, its anxious wanderings, begins the process of remembering," Pansy returns in memory to her childhood.[18] Recalling that at times in the past the world had seemed to her to be a single color—yellow one summer, green one spring—she wonders whether it had ever been pink. "She could not be sure and she did not care. Of one thing she was certain: never had the world enclosed her before and never had the quiet been so smooth" (*CS*, 193). The doctor, the symbol of the patriarchy, violates Pansy's sanctum, purloins her se-

18. *Ibid.*

cret treasure. "You are a thief," she tells him silently. "You are heartless and you should be put to death." But she admits, as Stafford's intelligent female heroes inevitably do, that "the time would come when she could no longer live in seclusion, she must go into the world again" (*CS*, 192).

It is a briefer and therefore less dangerous withdrawal that Cora Savage experiences in "The Philosophy Lesson." Like Jean Stafford, Cora earns money for college by working as an art students' model. The students marvel at her "inhuman" ability to remain still for long periods of time. Cora is held in her position by the scene outside the studio window of a cottonwood tree, every leaf and branch of which she knows so well "that she still saw it, if her mind's eye wandered" (*CS*, 362). This day, as Cora poses, snow (which she loves because it "forever conceal[s] the harshness of the world") begins to fall, and with the students busy at their work, she is gratified that only she notices: "For the time being, the snow was a private experience; perhaps everything at this moment proceeded from her own mind" (*CS*, 364, 365). She remembers from her philosophy course Bishop Berkeley, who maintained that reality is an idea in the mind of God, and "she concluded that she would be at peace forever if she could believe that she existed only for herself and possibly a superior intelligence and that no one existed for her save when he was tangibly present" (*CS*, 365).

Inevitably, the world outside herself, in the form of the news of a student's suicide, intrudes into Cora's reverie and forces her back to reality. Like Clarissa Dalloway in her fleeting communion with Septimus Warren Smith in Virginia Woolf's *Mrs. Dalloway*, Cora experiences a transitory moment of understanding of the dead student, whom she knows slightly. Then, finally, she recognizes that her desire to exist by and for herself is futile.

> And what was the misery that had brought the boy to suicide? Rich, privileged, in love, he . . . had seemed the very paradigm of joy. Why had he done it? And yet, why not? Why did not she, who was so seldom happy, do it herself? A darkness beat her like the wings of an enormous bird and frantic terror of the ultimate hopelessness shook her until the staff she held slipped and her heart seemed for a moment to fail. . . . The bell rang and her pole went clattering to the floor, knocking over a portrait on an easel nearby, and all the students, still talking of the death that morning, looked up with exclamations of shock, but she could

tell by their faces that none of them had been thinking her thoughts, that she alone, silent and stationary there on the dais, had shared Bernard Allen's experience and plunged with him into sightlessness. No. No, wait a minute. Each mortal in the room must, momentarily, have died. But just as the fledgling artists put their own faces on their own canvases, so they had perished in their own particular ways.

The snow was a benison. It forgave them all. (*CS*, 369)

With "Beatrice Trueblood's Story" Stafford continues her exploration of the oppressions of marriage for women and complicates her investigation of mental instability by presenting the complementary complications of physical illness. "When Beatrice Trueblood was in her middle thirties and on the very eve of her second marriage to a rich and reliable man—when, that is, she was in the prime of life and on the threshold of a rosier phase of it than she had ever known before," the story begins, "she overnight was stricken with total deafness" (*CS*, 385). Priscilla Onslager, Beatrice's sprightly Newport hostess and friend, curses the fates who have attacked Beatrice just as she is escaping her horrid childhood and devastating first marriage. But Priscilla's husband, Jack, who talks less and observes more than his wife, the night before the mysterious tragedy witnessed a quarrel between Beatrice and Marten ten Brink, her fiancé, that convinces him that Beatrice is not as happy as her friends insist she must be: "He heard not a word of it—not at the dance, that is—and he saw not a gesture or a grimace of anger, but he nevertheless knew surely, as he watched them dance together, that ten Brink was using every ounce of his strength not to shout, and to keep in check a whole menagerie of passions—fire-breathing dragons and bone-crushing serpents and sabertoothed tigers—and he knew also that Beatrice was running for dear life against the moment when they would be unleashed, ready to gobble her up" (*CS*, 390). Later in the evening Jack does hear the end of the engaged couple's altercation: "'You mustn't think you can shut your mind to these things,' he said. 'You can't shut your ears to them.' Their voices were clear in the hush of the last of the night. 'I am exhausted with talk, Marten,' said Beatrice softly. 'I will not hear another word'" (*CS*, 392).

When Beatrice discovers her deafness the following day, she breaks her engagement ("she didn't want to be a burden") and returns to New York, where doctors agree that her deafness is not physiological (*CS*, 387). Her friends send Jack to convince her to consult a psychoanalyst, and he finds his friend content in her silent world, and "as proud and secret-living as a flower" (*CS*, 393). Beatrice admits to Jack that she chose to hear no more. Having grown up, like Sonie Marburg, the innocent audience of her parents' splenetic and acidulous arguments, Beatrice as a child had often "imagined herself alone on a desert, far away from any human voice" (*CS*, 402). In an effort to escape her wrangling parents, at twenty-one she had married Tom Trueblood, a man "sustained by rancor and contentiousness," who "scolded her for seven years" (*CS*, 403, 402).

Becoming deaf, she confesses to Jack, was a coward's attempt to break off her engagement with Marten ten Brink, an "indefatigably vocal" man with whom life was "an incessant wrangle" (*CS*, 401). Indeed, Beatrice confides, she had wished for silence, but "she had not bargained for banishment . . . she had only wanted a holiday. Now, though, she felt that the Devil lived with her, eternally wearing a self-congratulatory smile" (*CS*, 400). Deafness, she explains, is egocentric, and she confesses, in her loneliness, that she regrets her wish. Beatrice eventually sees a psychiatrist and regains her hearing, and marries a poor research chemist. The newlyweds visit the Onslagers, and when Priscilla "exclaimed after the second evening that she had never seen Beatrice so radiant, Onslager agreed with her. Why not? There would be no sense in quarreling with his happy wife. He himself had never seen a face so drained of joy, or even of the memory of joy; he had not been able to meet Bea's eyes" (*CS*, 404). Like Evan Leckie in "The Maiden," who betrays his traditional, unenlightened attitudes toward women throughout the story—in his scorn of the WACs in Nuremburg as "modern mutations" of women and in his admiration of Frau Reinmuth because she lives not only for but through her husband—Jack Onslager is a (rare) sympathetic male character, who nonetheless exposes his true ideas about women when he finds silent Beatrice "the embodiment of everything most pricelessly feminine" (*CS*, 399).

Like Cora Savage Maybank and Beatrice Trueblood, many of Jean Stafford's other characters escape the difficulties and disappointments of their lives in physical maladies. Stafford explains her fascination with illness, perhaps inadvertently, in "The Psychological Novel," when she states that "we are confronted by wars and the wickedness that makes them, and the famine and *disease* and spiritual mutilations that follow them, by the shipwreck of our manners and our morality, by an almost universal *sickness* of heart." The last metaphor is, of course, appropriate. In *The American Short Story* William Peden discusses Stafford's fiction (along with that of Tennessee Williams, Carson McCullers, Flannery O'Connor, and other "New Gothic" writers) in a chapter entitled "Sick in Mind and Body." The "smell of the sick room permeates the thoughtful, carefully wrought stories of Jean Stafford," Peden writes. "With very few exceptions physical maladies, individual peculiarities, or private misfortunes force her characters to withdraw from the world of customary urges and responses into a sick world of unfulfilled longings and desires." [19]

Certainly Stafford's characters' ailments, both physical and mental, are metaphors for the modern human being's alienation from society. Yet the theme is particularly appropriate for Stafford's cast of female characters. Social scientists and historians have in recent years examined the relationship between women's position in our society and the prevalence of certain types of illness among women. Eating disorders like anorexia and bulimia; agoraphobia and claustrophobia; aphasia and amnesia; rheumatoid arthritis, and other emotion-affected diseases are particularly common among women. And, as Gilbert and Gubar note, there is in literature a long tradition of delineation of the collateral themes of women and illness. In their analysis of the complementary images in literature of woman as angel and monster, they assert that "it is debilitating to be any woman in a society where women are warned that if they do not behave like angels they must be monsters." A young woman, observe Gilbert and Gubar, "is likely to experience her education in docility, submissiveness, self-lessness as in some ways sickening. To be trained in renunciation is almost necessarily to be trained in ill health, since the human animal's first and strongest urge is to his/her *own* survival, pleasure, assertion." [20] Jean Stafford, herself a notorious hypochondriac who nonetheless genuinely suffered from a variety of illnesses throughout her adulthood, examines the typically feminine escape into illness from the anxieties of life.

"The Warlock," like "Beatrice Trueblood's Story," presents a self-

19. Stafford, "The Psychological Novel," 223–24, italics mine; Peden, *American Short Story*, 98–99.
20. Gilbert and Gubar, *Madwoman in the Attic*, 54.

aware character who ruminates on the motivations and repercussions of her ill health. Recuperating from "a long and depressing illness" and an operation, Marianne Kimball foregoes the pressures of a family Christmas for a cruise to the West Indies. Mrs. Kimball is "tired nearly to death" and she wants to be alone in her recovery: "Her nerves were fitful, and there was a chill like the mortal chill of old age, that lay in the marrow of her bones; she wanted to lie, still and warm and silent, by herself and wait, as a patient animal waits, for her renascence." Interestingly, Mrs. Kimball does not doubt that she is "on the mend," no doubt because the suspected cause of her illness has disappeared.

> Just before her illness, she and Mark Kimball had been on the very brink of divorce, and while they were now at peace and safe again, she felt that never could she be sure whether it had been pity for her in her weakness and fear or the restitution of his married love that had brought him back to her from a long and serious digression. Nor—and this was even worse—could she be sure that her illness, coming at a time so crucial, had not been unconscious blackmail; it was almost, she thought, as if her body itself had said to Mark, "See, if you leave me for Martha, I will die!" Marianne Kimball, an honest woman, could not bear these days to hear the word "psychosomatic."[21]

Like Pansy Vanneman, Cora Maybank, Beatrice Trueblood—and Jean Stafford—Marianne Kimball recognizes that physical illness is related, even if unconsciously, to one's emotional and mental well-being: "Some part of her mind, she was sure, had been awake in the operating room while the rest of her had been killed violently with ether, and this unforgiving and unforgetting self could sometimes prejudice the rest of her and persuade her that she was a scapegoat and a victim."[22] And, in her perception that "her body itself" has taken control, she recognizes that, as Katharine Congreve's experience demonstrates, the will is a formidable component of one's personality; as one of Beatrice Trueblood's more insightful friends articulates, "The will is free and very strong . . . [but] it can cease to become an agent and become a despot" (CS, 397).

Mrs. Kimball survives her sojourn on the shabby ship, as well as harassment by her inexorably cheerful cabin-mate and the ship's

21. Jean Stafford, "The Warlock," New Yorker, December 24, 1955, pp. 25, 27–28.
22. Ibid., 30, 33, 44.

ubiquitous doctor, and an attack of influenza that leaves her wondering whether she was "faltering into permanent invalidism." When her husband wires that he is flying to join her at her port, she rejoices in "her release from gloomy caverns and her return to the blue-skied world."[23] Like many of her stories, "The Warlock" betrays Stafford's acceptance of the stereotypes of male-female relationships; it is a man, her husband, who inspires Marianne Kimball's return to her life as a wife and mother. Yet again Stafford's message is life affirming. The protagonist whose inertia and fear send her, at the beginning of the story, to a holiday away from friends and family, finally rejects her solipsism and poor health for a return to normalcy.

One of Stafford's best-known stories, "Children Are Bored on Sunday," similarly explores the relationship between mental and physical illness, and the temptations and ultimate limitations of a withdrawal from the outside world. Somewhat inexplicably, Stafford tells us less about the protagonist of this story than about most of her characters. For Emma she provides no surname and no age, and we know of her origins only that she spent at least part of her childhood on a farm. She is obviously not at home in the story's New York setting. Indeed, Emma's alienation from the artsy, cosmopolitan crowd with whom she travels is the salient fact of the story. In this story it is, not the hero's husband or social restrictions that inspire her collapse, but her inability to function in the intellectual, male community in which she finds herself. Emma is mesmerized and perplexed by the metropolitan intellectuals ("Olympians," she calls them) whose childhood experiences were, she reflects, so dissimilar to hers. She originally pities the urbanites who had not enjoyed a carefree rural childhood of cats and Charles Dickens, but later wonders "who was she to patronize and pity them? Her own childhood, rich as it seemed to her on reflection, had not equipped her to read, or to see, or to listen, as theirs had done; she envied them and despised them at the same time, and at the same time she feared and admired them" (*CS*, 376).

Emma is painfully aware of her position in this society. While not an intellectual, neither is she—because she has been college-educated—a legitimate rube: "Neither staunchly primitive nor confidently *au courant*, she rarely knew where she was at. And this was

---

23. *Ibid.*, 33, 44.

her Achilles' heel: her identity was always mistaken, and she was thought to be an intellectual who, however, had not made the grade. It was no use now to cry that she was not, that she was a simon-pure rube; not a soul would believe her. She knew, deeply and with horror, that she was thought merely stupid" (*CS*, 378).

Under the strain of her anomalous life, some months before the time of the story Emma began to break down—walking for hours in a desperate attempt to become tired enough to sleep at night; drinking, but, in her own manifestation of women's eating disorders, eating only the slightest amounts of repellent food; finally closing the door of her mental tomb. Now it is a Sunday in winter, and a trip to the Metropolitan Museum of Art is her first hesitant venture into the outside world. She spies Alfred Eisenburg, a gaunt Olympian (she was uncertain if he was a writer, a painter, or a composer, "but his specialty did not matter, for his larger designation was that of 'the intellectual'") whom she likes and with whom she had flirted briefly at a party (*CS*, 378). The sight of one of the intimidating group unnerves her, and she decides that her "excursion into the world is premature; her solitude must continue for a while, and perhaps it would never end . . . she wasn't fit to be seen. Although she was no longer mutilated, she was still unkempt; her pretensions needed brushing; her ambiguities needed to be cleaned; her evasions would have to be completely overhauled" (*CS*, 377). Articulating Stafford's belief in the interdependence of emotional and physical illness, Emma, as she wanders through the galleries, muses upon the "sick at heart": "Between herself and the canvases swam the months of spreading, cancerous distrust, of anger that made her seasick, of grief that shook her like an influenza chill, of the physical afflictions by which the poor victimized spirit sought vainly to wreck the arrogantly healthy flesh" (*CS*, 381).

Suddenly remembering, however, that she has heard that Eisenburg has suffered too—a divorce, the loss of a job, poverty—Emma longs to approach her acquaintance, "her cousin-german in the territory of despair," and propose a "painful communion" of "their invalid souls," a "honeymoon of the cripples . . . [a] nuptial consummation of the abandoned." She recognizes that "only thus, as sick people, could they marry. In any other terms, it would be a *mesalliance*, doomed to divorce from the start, for rubes and intellectuals must stick to their own class" (*CS*, 382, 381). Incredibly, but inevitably, the sick people in their "mutual necessity" meet, and Eisenburg recognizes that their suffering can—however briefly—be shared. They go off together to an out-of-the-way bar, and the story concludes:

> Actually, there was nothing to fear; even if they had heard catcalls or if someone had hooted at them, "Intellectual loves Rube!" they would have been impervious, for the heart carved in the bark of the apple tree would contain the names Emma and Alfred, and there were no perquisites to such a conjugation. To her own heart, which was shaped exactly like a valentine, there came a winglike palpitation, a delicate exigency, and all the fragrance of all the flowery springtime love affairs that ever were seemed waiting for them in the whisky bottle. To mingle their pain, their handshake promised them, was to produce a separate entity, like a child that could shift for itself, and they scrambled toward this profound and pastoral experience. (*CS*, 383)

This is no "happily-ever-after" story; a drink is only a drink, and Emma and Alfred have only a winter Sunday afternoon "to play together, quite naked, quite innocent" (*CS*, 382). In Stafford's world a transitory moment of communion is the most that the battered and outcast can hope for. But the interaction, however brief it inevitably is in a discontinuous and disillusioning world, is preferable to the solitude and silent suffering of illness. When the entente is withheld, when the sickness remains untreated and the suffering unassuaged, the withdrawal is unavoidable.

One of Stafford's most haunting studies of female behavior and mental illness is "The Echo and the Nemesis," whose protagonist is among her most memorable and unique characters. A serious student of philology, Ramona Dunn appears to her friend Sue to be confident and erudite. Arrogant and self-possessed, Ramona sports a pair of binoculars through which she looks "through the wrong end . . . liking, for some reason that she did not disclose, to diminish the world she surveyed"; and her unusual clothes, though expensive, are mismatched and dirty, clothing a body that is "fat to the point of parody" (*CS*, 37, 36). Because she is shy and, studying at Heidelberg University, far from home, the more conventional Sue Ledbetter has befriended her eccentric American colleague and suddenly, some months after they have met, learns that her strange friend is rich; that the members of her family now live in Italy; that they are all (except Ramona) handsome and happy; and that her deceased twin sister,

Martha, had been the most beautiful and splendid of all. As Ramona talks about her cosmopolitan family, she "changed before Sue's eyes; from the envelope of fat emerged a personality as *spirituelle* and knowing as any practicing sophisticate's," and when she suggests that Sue come to Italy for Christmas to meet her brothers, the homesick girl is thrilled (*CS*, 41).

As her friend embroiders on the story of her family and her past, and recalls how thin and beautiful she had been as a child, Sue is astounded to learn that Ramona has not always been fat, and pities the pathetic girl who will undoubtedly never regain her lost beauty and happiness. Ramona continues her confidences, telling Sue what it is to be "the unhappiest girl in the world," to be "ruled by food and half driven out of one's mind until one dreamed of it and had at last no other ambition but to eat incessantly with an appetite that grew and grew until one saw oneself, in nightmares, as nothing but an enormous mouth and a tongue, trembling lasciviously" (*CS*, 42–43). Confessing that she has come to Heidelberg, not to study, but to lose weight so that she can return to her family proudly, Ramona convinces Sue to help her, to act as her conscience and keep her from eating. Sue pursues her role as watchdog assiduously, but Ramona occasionally lapses, and when, with remorse for having gorged herself on a dozen cherry tarts, Ramona puts out a cigarette on her own wrist, confused Sue begins to watch her friend more closely. As the holidays grow near, Ramona becomes querulous and elusive; "she acquired the notion that people were staring at her, and she carried an umbrella, rain or shine, to hide herself from them" (*CS*, 47). One day Ramona suddenly decides that Sue is the exact image of her twin, Martha, and that since her brothers would be shocked by the resemblance, they cannot go to Italy for their vacation.

Ramona's behavior grows increasingly bizarre. She calls Sue "Martha, Sister, Twin," and fluctuates between rages against her family and especially "Martha, that ghastly, puling, pampered hypochondriac who had totally wrecked her life," and protestations that her family is really "good and kind. The only thing that's true," she confesses, "is that I eat all the time" (*CS*, 48, 49). Finally, Ramona announces that since the experiment of living alone in Heidelberg has failed, her father is coming to take her home. She invites Sue for the first time to her rooms, to eat the contraband food that is hidden there. Sue sees a photo of Martha and, suspecting that the picture is really of Ramona, turns it over to read the penned inscription, "'Martha Ramona Dunn at sixteen, Sorrento.' She looked at that ethereal face again, and this time had no doubt that it had once belonged to Ramona. No wonder the loss of it had left her heartbroken! She sighed to think of her friend's desperate fabrication. In a sense, she supposed the Martha side of Ramona Dunn *was* dead, dead and buried under layers and layers of fat" (*CS*, 51).

During the afternoon, Ramona gorges herself on the sweets: "Shamelessly, she ranged up and down the table, cropping and lowing like a cow in the pasture. There were droplets of sweat on her forehead and her hands were shaking, but nothing else about her showed that she had gone to pieces earlier or that she was deep, deeper by far than anyone else Sue had ever known," (*CS*, 51–52). Eventually Ramona admits that, of course, Sue does not look like Martha, and explains that she is "'exceptionally ill.' She spoke with pride, as if she were really saying 'I am exceptionally talented' or 'I am exceptionally attractive'" (*CS*, 52). When Sue somewhat feebly expresses sorrow, Ramona protests: "*I'm* not sorry. It is for yourself that you should be sorry. You have such a trivial little life, poor girl. It's not your fault. Most people do. . . . Of *course* you could never know the divine joy of being twins, provincial one!" (*CS*, 52).

"The Echo and the Nemesis" is Stafford's intriguingly ironic variation on traditionally feminine fantasies "in which maddened doubles function as asocial surrogates for docile selves." The twin motif of *Boston Adventure*, in which the "angel" Sonie is juxtaposed with her alter ego, the "monster" Hopewell, is inverted, and Ramona, reacting against her life of submission as the pampered, weak Martha, becomes instead a robust, intellectual grotesque who exchanges physical dependency for mental instability. "Learning to become a beautiful object," Gilbert and Gubar write, "the girl learns anxiety about— perhaps even loathing of—her own flesh." Female characters manifest their aversion to their bodies in a variety of eating disorders, from, in "Children Are Bored on Sunday," Emma's self-destructive, anorexic refusal to eat at all, to Ramona's example, "an 'outbreak' that transforms . . . characters into huge and powerful monsters."[24]

24. Gilbert and Gubar, *Madwoman in the Attic*, xi, 54, 86.

Unlike Emma, Beatrice, and Mrs. Kimball, Ramona is irrevocably lost, and Stafford leaves us to wonder, at the story's denouement, whether poor innocent Sue's horrified flight from her dinner is a rejection of the aberrant overeating that has destroyed Ramona, or an equally dangerous repudiation of any nourishment at all.

Stafford's fascination with women's displaced reactions against their alienation and humans' response to the afflictions of postwar society is reflected throughout her stories in minor characters that experience the illness and pain that plague all human beings. Many of her stories deal with the elderly and their inevitable physical maladies. "Life Is No Abyss," "The Bleeding Heart," and "Old Flaming Youth" present cogent portraits of the exigencies of old age. In other stories, like "The Echo and the Nemesis," in which Sue and Ramona eat in an old ladies' home where "withered lips" squawk in "protest against the dreary lot of being old and homeless and underfed," the loneliness and poverty of old age offer metaphorical comment on the loneliness and poverty of the lives of all those who live on the edge of society. Throughout Stafford's stories, imagery underscores the theme of suffering. In "The Home Front," for example, Dr. Pakheiser avoids involving himself with his fellow transients in a wartime boardinghouse and strives to make his own room like a home, for "had he not done so, he, too, probably would have wandered from one boarding house to the next like a sick person constantly shifting about in his bed trying to find a comfortable position for his aching bones" (*CABS*, 108). In an extended analogy, Stafford, in "The Children's Game," introduces a Belgian casino "that could have been a hospital ward save that the uniform was dinner dress, not *deshabille*. . . . Everyone in the warm, bland, airless room . . . looked chronically ill and engrossed with his symptoms. And while the symptoms might vary, the malady was the same. . . . The common denominator . . . was that of the invalid concentrating on the tides of his pain, a look necessarily unsociable" (*CS*, 19). And Stafford reminds us that love, though painful, is not terminal, when in "A Slight Maneuver," the young lovers, Theo and Clyde, are manipulated by his divorced aunt, who "had been stricken like themselves and had recovered so well that she could not remember what the pain had been like."[25]

25. Jean Stafford, "A Slight Maneuver," *Mademoiselle*, XXIV (February, 1947), 205.

Many of Jean Stafford's stories present her interpretation of a world in which the anxieties of interpersonal relations evoke in people—women especially—a variety of responses: fear, bitterness, sorrow, sickness, madness. Underlying the personal reactions of her characters is the fundamental, reprehensible inclination to withdraw from life, to relinquish one's responsibilities to one's self and others. Stafford's characters are doomed or saved by their self-awareness and their willingness to risk pain and suffering; Angelica Early's naïveté and Jenny Peck's fear are fatal and debilitating, but Emma, Marianne Kimball, and Pansy Vanneman have at least a chance at a full, complex life.

In another group of stories, Stafford presents the coming-of-age of young female protagonists, those who, like Sonie Marburg and Molly Fawcett, are just discovering and reacting to the complexities of growing up female in modern American society. In these tales of initiation, young heroes confront experiences that result in a revelation and an accompanying loss of innocence. While lucky characters like Polly Bay and Cora Savage are changed by events, others are introduced to the bleak vision of a world in which knowledge is simply the recognition that "life is essentially a matter of being done in, let down, and swindled" (*CS*, 286).

The satire of "Maggie Meriwether's Rich Experience" characterizes one of Stafford's most delightful stories, which chronicles the increasing discomfiture of an American girl at a gathering of decadent Europeans in the French countryside. Maggie Meriwether is young and homesick, and her estrangement is underscored by the cruel fact that "her French, acquired easily and then polished painstakingly at Sweet Briar, had forsaken her absolutely the very moment the Channel boat docked in Calais, and while, to her regret and often to her bitter abasement, she had understood almost everything she had heard since she had been in France, she had not been able to utter a word" (*CS*, 4). A British companion, Tippy Akenside, entices Maggie to join the continental group by promising that everyone would speak English at the picnic, since "English was ever so smart these days." But English was not being spoken, "not even by—especially not by—Tippy," and Maggie is silent, over dressed, and miserable (*CS*, 5).

The sophisticated aristocrats suffer her presence with unnerving apathy, and Maggie does not know "whether she was invisible or whether she was an eyesore too excruciating to look at" (*CS*, 6). But even in her discomfort, she regrets that she is not enjoying her experience, which she knows is "a rich one for a simple country-club girl from Tennessee" (*CS*, 6). The setting, the luxurious Palladian estate of Karl von Bubnoff, M. le Baron, boasts a pool with black swans and acres of classical gardens, orchards, and vineyards. Lunch includes salmon and capon; artichokes and asparagus; melon and Brie; wine, champagne, and coffee. And the guests are a parodic cast of Jamesian aristocrats. They include small, swarthy, Greek Mme Floquet; "Amazonian" Mrs. Preston, a Russian with gold fingernails; and flashy Contessa Giovennazzo, all of whom admire each other's ostentatious jewels and compare favorite narcotics. And, with remarkable solidarity, they ignore Maggie Meriwether. The men, less colorful, include the bachelor Baron, feckless Tippy, and a mysterious Scottish buffoon named Serge, who "looked like a nearly penniless schoolmaster with dyspepsia and a tendency to catarrh" (*CS*, 11). The sophisticated women's aversion to Serge disposes Maggie, who recognizes a fellow outcast, to like him, and he turns out to be a rich Georgian prince with a colorful past.

Somehow Maggie survives her misadventure, and back at her hotel she finds flowers and a note from an American friend asking her to dine that evening with him and other friends. Grabbing the phone, she gets through "in rapid, rebellious French" and accepts the invitation. "The group of six who had dinner together that night were all Americans, and they loved Maggie's story, requiring her to repeat parts of it over again. . . . And they toasted Maggie Meriwether, the most sophisticated, the most cosmopolitan, and prettiest raconteur of middle Tennessee" (*CS*, 17).

"Maggie Meriwether's Rich Experience" is one of Stafford's most witty and acerbic stories. The juxtaposition of pretentious patricians, whose manners and mores she keenly observes, and the character of Maggie, the bedraggled, homesick compatriot of Stafford's "Innocents Abroad"—as Stafford entitled the opening section of her *Collected Stories*—creates a breezy comedy of manners that lightens the serious consideration of a young girl's coming-of-age.

More somber in tone than "Maggie Meriwether" is "The Mountain Day," similarly operating on two levels. The story's narrator and protagonist, New Yorker Judy Grayson, who spends every summer with her family in the mountains of Colorado, has this summer fallen in love with Rod Stephansson, a Harvard plant pathology student who is studying in Colorado. The story opens on a Sunday in August, a perfect mountain day—the air is still and clear; the sky a "cruel, infuriated blue" (*CS*, 239). The last two adjectives are salient, for throughout "The Mountain Day," Judy's naïvely cheerful narration is undercut by imagery and occurrences that belie her love-blind interpretation of her experience. Judy, who became engaged to Rod only the night before, is preoccupied with her fiancé and his perceptions of her. "For weeks, like a leaf turning constantly to the sun for its sustenance," she remarks, "so my whole existence had leaned toward Rod's recognition and approval of me, as if without them I would fade and wither. . . . Often, in the self-conceit of my love, I was so intent upon his image of me that I could not, for a moment, summon up an image of *him*" (*CS*, 231). Judy revels in the memory of the summer and her "storybook summertime romance. . . . Is there anything on earth more unearthly," she wonders dramatically, "than to be in love at eighteen?" (*CS*, 234, 236). Her euphoria remains as, later in the day, she and Rod join her sister and her sister's fiancé on horseback for a picnic on the mountain peak. "We had our lunch at the top of the world," she writes. "It was unquestionably the best meal I have ever eaten in my life" (*CS*, 242).

Surely such childish hyperbole is not to be taken seriously; Stafford's clever use of first-person past-tense narration allows her to convey meaning on two levels. Only a young person in love could utter such platitudes, and only a narrator looking back over the awareness of intervening years could clarify the author's attitude and tone with phrases like "in the self-conceit of my love" and "it was only years later that I was able to arrive at this analysis" (*CS*, 231, 232). With the advantage of hindsight, Judy can more realistically present the complexities of her experience.

Recalling the evening before, when Rod proposed, Judy notes that it "had started out badly." She perceives the unpleasantness of the political argument between her father and her sister's fiancé, and notes that her father's reaction was so violent "that you thought he might at any moment go and get a gun and shoot to kill" (*CS*, 236). The young couples escape to "a squalid, dusty honky-tonk in Puma, patronized by subhuman ne'er-do-wells and old wattled trollops who glared hostilely at us when we went in; at the bar an ugly customer, very drunk, spat on the floor as we walked by, and with feral hatred said, 'Goddam yearling dudes!'" (*CS*, 236).

The next day, the "perfect 'mountain day,'" the foursome ascends the mountain peak, gradually leaving behind the lake on which the red canoe floats bottom up, "like a bright, immaculate wound." It is "a wonderful lake—limpid, blue, shaped like a heart." And yet, "There were some horrid inhabitants of that lovely water, too—huge turtles and hellbenders, about which Davy [Judy's younger brother] had screaming nightmares" (*CS*, 239, 237). Love overwhelms Judy, who thinks youthfully that "everyone is happy today; this is the happiest day in the history of the world"; she and her comrades descend from their outing with "unshakable faith in our future lives" (*CS*, 242).

Such an attitude begs for enlightenment, and when, late in the day, the picnickers stop for a drink with Judy's grandmother, who summers nearby, they learn that her young Irish maids have not returned from their own picnic by the lake. The group searches casually, even cheerfully, for the pretty Irish girls who remind Judy of an "illustration in an old-fashioned romantic novel," until someone spots the canoe—which the maids, because they cannot swim, are forbidden to use—floating upside down on the water. As the others run for the motorboat, Judy follows up on a desperate hunch that the girls have gone to her house, and runs off alone, certain that she will find the lost maids and win her fiancé's admiration for her level-headedness. She stumbles, and the pain of a twisted ankle inspires her sad revelation that it is merely her selfish desire for Rod's approval that makes her want to find the women alive.

The maids have drowned, of course, and at the solemn family gathering later, Judy, given her first drink, feels grown up. Suddenly

> I found myself just then standing firmly on my own, and I was able to see everyone clearly—even myself. Earlier, in my blinding cocoon, when I had thought so constantly about Rod's respect for me, I had lost, in a sense, my respect for myself, but now, at last, I was able to think of *him* and not of his opinion of *me*. Bedraggled, my hair all wild, beggar's-lice on my sweater and my trousers, I did not care at all how I looked. I cared only, looking at the green pallor of his face, that he had suffered. I wanted him to be as happy as he had been before we had started our search for the girls, and I thought, Love, real love, is just that: it is

> wanting the beloved to be happy. The simplicity of the equation sur-
> prised me, but only for a moment and then it was incorporated into me
> as naturally as if it had been there all along. (*CS*, 249)

Judy's dramatic experience culminates in a revelation that teaches her about the sometimes sordid realities of life and the true nature of love. As always, Stafford's interest in her young characters' development as women is evident. When Judy perceives that her preoccupation with her fiancé's opinion of her undermines her sense of her own worth, she learns another valuable lesson about maturity and male-female relationships.

"The Darkening Moon," another tale in which the young protagonist's development is facilitated by a dramatic event, is a complex examination of the inevitabilities of aging, disillusionment, and compromise. Eleven-year-old Ella and her small mare, Squaw, are "ready for adventure" as they prepare to ride to Ella's babysitting job at a nearby ranch (*CS*, 252). If there is a moon or if snow distorts the bluffs on the dark road, Squaw is sometimes skittish during the trip to the Temples' ranch. But Ella looks forward to the ride and, though she is late, slows Squaw to a trot as she nears the Temples', for "she wanted to postpone as long as possible the moment when she would go into the house" (*CS*, 253–54).

Like Molly, and like many other female heroes, Ella is comfortable in the openness and freedom of nature. Her father, dead only a year, had taught her as a young girl that there is nothing to fear in the open air, and so long as she is outdoors, she is not afraid at night. Inside, however, Ella is terrified of the slightest sound or movement, and spends her evenings at the Temples' cowering in a chair and counting the minutes until she can be safely outside again: "The clock was in the kitchen, but she had not the courage to go through the dining room, across the creaking floor of the pantry, into the spacious kitchen, where not even bright daylight dispelled the gloomy shadows cast by large cabinets and by the many chaps hanging along one wall" (*CS*, 257).

This night, however, the darkness outside is eerie. The mountains loom "like the blurred figures of fantastic beasts," and the animals are restless. A cow loudly mourns her recently butchered calf, and the horses, running aimlessly, punctuate the silence with "lunatic neighs" (*CS*, 251, 257). When she hears a horse kicking Squaw, Ella runs outside to intervene and "to her amazement, saw that there was a full moon overhead. It was as large as a harvest moon, as pale as lard. There had been no moon when she rode down, nor even moon sign" (*CS*, 258). Several minutes later, after she ties up her horse, Ella notices that "the moon was a little smaller than it had been," and although still large, it gives little light (*CS*, 258). The moon continues to disappear, and when Ella's "sharp eyes sought clouds to explain the phenomenon they found nothing but the moon in the black vault" (*CS*, 259).

Ella returns to the house and resumes her countdown, but she is distracted by the uncanny silence. The bereaved cow is quiet now, the horses and owls are still, and each time she looks at the moon "a little more had dwindled away" (*CS*, 259). Inexplicably, the lantern-lighted room that had earlier seemed garish now has a "warm, saffron glow," and "for the first time, she reflected that it was an elegant room" (*CS*, 259). Creeping out into the silence, Ella watches as the moon blackens and wonders, "Were all the creatures waiting, like her, for the final disappearance of the moon and the disaster that would follow it?" (*CS*, 260). Total darkness and an owl's sudden cry chase terrified Ella back into the house. The shadows of the bookshelves loom, in the dying lantern light, like cattails at the river where her father had taught her about nature.

> The water had been cold and once she had slipped and fallen in up to her waist. The fish were so thick that they swarmed slimily over her and she had nearly gagged at the smell. "Bring me them on the bank there," her father had said and she had had to pick up the fat slithering blobs in her bare hands. Her father, reaching out to take them, had smeared her wrist with fish's blood which dripped in gouts from his fingertips as if it were his own. Even if he were still alive and asked her, she would not go there again! The memory for some reason, though it was only a memory of a time long ago, made her start to cry. (*CS*, 261)

The reason, though Ella is too young to recognize it, just as she is too young to understand the eclipse, is that nature—and the world—have betrayed her. The five-year-old memory of a pleasant fishing excursion with her father becomes, at adolescence, a threatening flashback of a childhood world that the adolescent, acculturated, female Ella must reject. Her tears are a young woman's mourning for the freedom that she must abandon if she is to survive as a woman in the world. The outside world has become dark and threatening, the suddenly genteel interior safe and comforting. When the Temples return to frightened Ella and Mr. Temple disparages the usually intrepid girl's fear, his wife's retort is Stafford's thesis: "It's a funny thing. Works backward with some people, you might say. Some way, as you get older . . . I don't know. I'm just thinking the way I used to be. Until I was fifteen, wasn't a living thing could give me a turn. And then, later on . . ." (*CS*, 262). All of us grow up to the knowledge that life is disappointing and often betrays. But it is most often women, who, with maturity, learn to doubt themselves, to compromise their dreams, to live with fear and anxiety, to feel comfortable in elegant interiors. "They grow up to a point . . . and then they '[grow] down.'"[26] It is a wiser but sadder Ella who rides home with her eyes closed, and "a world slipped past her blinded eyes as she traversed a road she would not recognize again, beneath the full, unfaithful moon" (*CS*, 262).

In "A Winter's Tale," Stafford abandons her familiar epiphanic technique for a more deliberate, leisurely revelation. As the story begins, Fanny, the narrator and protagonist, has some days before discovered in an attic a quilted jacket that she has not worn since she was twenty and spent a winter in Heidelberg. Putting on the jacket, Fanny finds herself transported back seventeen years and enveloped by a "mood that for some days now I have received like a speechless and ghostly visitor whenever I am alone," a mood that inspires memories of a "winter of my youth, irrelevant to all my present situations, a half-year so sharply independent of all my later history that I read it like a fiction; or like a dream in which all action is instinctive and none of it has its genesis in a knowledge of right and wrong" (*BC*, 226). The mood and memories are seductive, and Fanny knows that now, all of these years later, she has to return to that winter of youth.

Thus ends the frame story for the tale that follows, the story of a young Catholic American girl sent by her father to Germany for a year of study. Fanny, who is looking forward to her "first emancipation from Daddy" and a pastoral life of "waltzing, wine festivals and pleasure steamers on the Rhine," is instead entrusted to the care of a family friend, Persis Galt, a Bostonian convert to Catholicism who is married to a professor at the university (*BC*, 232, 252). Middle-aged,

26. Morgan, "Humanbecoming," in *Images of Women in Fiction: Feminist Perspectives*, 184.

attractive, physically fit Persis takes her job as surrogate parent seriously, arranging for Fanny to live at a pension where it will be convenient for her to attend daily Mass, and Fanny instantly dislikes the older woman. "All the time we were exchanging trifling information we were appraising each other and doing so as if we were contemporaries. I stopped feeling like a girl and felt like a woman; an immediate antipathy between us made me wary and adult. Never before and never since have I known this sheer and feral experience of instantly disliking and being disliked by another woman for no reason more substantial than that we were both women" (*BC*, 234). Persis recognizes and shares the feeling. "We don't really see eye to eye, do we?" she asks Fanny (*BC*, 238).

The chameleonlike Persis (who appears in various calculated guises—in the "tweeds and brogans" of a German matron when she meets Fanny's train, in a provocative black-velvet gown for tea) presides at tea over a group of monks, her husband's students, and assorted Storm Troopers and Blackshirts. Her entourage includes her "own personal monk," Dom Paternus; Mellie Anderson, a young girl who, like Fanny, has been entrusted to Persis' care and who informs Fanny that the woman's spies are everywhere; and Max Rossler, a handsome young soldier who looks "like the Devil" and whose face "expressed nothing" (*BC*, 249).

At Persis' instructions, Fanny is escorted to her nemesis' social events by Herr Rossler (who, Mellie claims, is Persis' "Number One spy"), and falls in love with the "false and enigmatic man, the deathless archetype that figured in the dreams of all masochistic schoolgirls" (*BC*, 247, 255). She knows that Rossler is attracted to her as well and wonders why he does not demonstrate his feelings, until the night he wearily confides the "stale, sad tale" that has caused him to hate Persis (*BC*, 258). At eighteen, five years earlier, he had been her husband's student, was seduced by the decadent woman, and is now enslaved by her knowledge of his secret past. Rossler warns Fanny to avoid him and trouble, and the girl recognizes immediately that it is to be "an intolerable love affair, raddled and strangled with our knowledge of its end. . . . There was no pleasure in it, I suffered perpetually, it was monstrous to live through, but I could not have escaped it, not possibly" (*BC*, 261, 262).

The fated affair drags on until Christmas, which Max and Fanny spend in Freiburg (where he gives her the quilted jacket). Max then informs her that he is going to Spain to fight. He tells her too the terrible secret that has enabled Persis to blackmail him: he is a Jew— in the late thirties, in Germany. Max is killed in Spain, and eventually Persis confronts Fanny with her knowledge of the affair. "She had come, craven, to drive a bargain with me: we would keep each other's secrets. I agreed although I did not give a damn. She was in her masquerade of tweeds and I pitied her immensely. My father died that May in Paris and I came back to Boston and my aunts" (*BC*, 275). Here the story shifts back to the present; it is two weeks later, and the gray February weather has turned warm. "I am exalted," Fanny writes. "I believe that I am altogether purged . . . my God, Jew or not he was a Nazi; and then I think, what did Nazi mean when I was twenty? So, finding no reason for preserving my guilt, I watch it give up the ghost" (*BC*, 276).

Fanny's recognition that the teaching experiences of life are not sinful, not based "in a knowledge of right and wrong," places her in the company of Stafford's more perceptive female heroes. A similar revelation and salvation are sustained by Theo in "A Slight Maneuver." Like Judy Grayson, a New Yorker summering in Colorado, Theo has spent her vacation with her fiancé and his aunt at her dude ranch. For Theo's last day, "Clyde's Aunt Naomi, a manly woman [who] paddled everyone's canoe," decides that the couple should visit the Carlsbad Caverns. Theo would prefer to spend the day leisurely, but since she is a guest and not a little intimidated by her imposing future in-law, she doesn't protest. She does, however, wonder why Clyde doesn't stand up to his guardian, and the incident casts him in a different light: "She considered him . . . not as the person with whom she was in love and who had rarely failed to delight her, but as the person she was going to marry, and . . . she resolved . . . to prolong her engagement. She realized with surprise and disappointment that his will-lessness with his aunt was transformed, when he was with her, into a firmness which might in time become bullying."[27]

The next day, in the "primeval blackness" of the "vast gruesome cavity," Theo's resentment against the older woman seethes. When she complains that Naomi has recommended the wrong shoes, Clyde

27. Stafford, "A Slight Maneuver," 177, 289.

becomes angry and, to Theo's dismay, looks just like his aunt. Later, Theo's anger shifts to its appropriate object, Clyde, and she "realized that she had gone quite beyond vexation, that she was extremely angry, that Clyde was weak and that he valued her happiness less than peace with his aunt." Four trying hours later, the tour of the caverns concludes with a male chorus singing "Lead, Kindly Light" in the resonant darkness, and Theo's response ironically echoes Mrs. Moore's reaction to the Marabar Caves in E. M. Forster's *Passage to India:* "The shock was maiming. Theo could see nothing, feel nothing, think nothing, desire nothing. The molehill became a mountain; she so disliked Clyde that she could not remember ever having liked him and she could not imagine what had got into her when she agreed to marry him." Neither Clyde nor Theo articulates, when he sees her onto the train, the fact of which each of them is aware—that this is their "final goodbye." [28]

Theo recognizes that her horrifying meeting with nothingness in the dark void of the cavern is precisely the experience that Naomi Heath, in her "brilliant subconscious mind," knows and plans that she will have. Clyde's aunt is, like Persis Galt, a fundamentally evil character, but the reader cannot but suspect that her breakup of Theo and Clyde's affair will ultimately work in Theo's favor. The girl who stoically accepts Clyde's decision to honor his aunt's wishes and visit the caverns because "he was the master, it was his decision," is not the woman who calmly departs forever from her fiancé. [29]

The insights experienced by Judy Grayson and Theo bring apparently real and lasting changes in their lives; for other of Stafford's young female characters, the prospects of growing up female in American culture are more bleak. Kitty Winstanley, in "The Tea Time of Stouthearted Ladies," counts the days before she can escape her mother's boardinghouse and return to her summer job as waitress and chambermaid at nearby Caribou ranch. Her stay at the ranch, with its hard, demeaning work, is not the vacation that Kitty's mother imagines, but it is at least preferable to life at home, where she must serve the college students who by day are colleagues in class. [30] The

28. *Ibid.*, 289.
29. *Ibid.*, 289, 285.
30. During the Great Depression, Stafford worked at her mother's boardinghouse in Boulder, and at a dude ranch, and writes cogently in "Souvenirs of Survival" of the trials of being a "Barbarian," of being "exhausted from classes and study and part-time jobs and perpetually starved for status . . . and clothes . . . and fun" (*CS*, 224).

students, whatever their hardships, confront reality; their beleaguered and deluded parents keep up a front, "saw the funny side of things" and "never said die" (*CS*, 220).

Out-of-work or tubercular husbands and fathers escape their weary wives' recriminations to long days in the park; returning home only for an early dinner, they are "fed like dogs in the kitchen, and then, like dogs, they disappeared" (*CS*, 224). Overworked wives and mothers, the nesters, turn their domestic instincts to employment and play mother to countless college students more affluent than their own children, and console each other in "imitation tea parties," where they "glibly evaluate the silver lining of the cloud beneath which they and their families lived, gasping for every breath" (*CS*, 220). The women lead vicarious lives: they discuss their boarders, not their own children; they avoid reference to personal problems, mentioning neither money nor disappointment nor "their hopeless, helpless contempt for their unemployed husbands. . . . Formal, fearful of intimacy lest the full confrontation with reality shatter them to smithereens," they ferociously conceal "the cancer [that] was invisible, deep in their broken, bleeding hearts" (*CS*, 220, 221).

The daylight allows illusions, but in the "bitter caverns" of the night Kitty, like Sonie Marburg, is the reluctant audience for her parents' "static diatribes" (*CS*, 222). Her mother accuses; her father, convinced that he is lazy, ineffectual, unmanly, does not defend himself. And Kitty, hating her father's silence and weakness ("once she had seen him cry when a small roof-repairing job that he had counted on was given to someone else, and she had wanted to die for disgust") and her mother's unfairness, hates "herself for hating in them what they could not help" (*CS*, 222).

The ranch, therefore, with its exhausting work, is a welcome relief from the duplicity of life with her parents: Kitty is "wild with impatience . . . to get away from home, from the spectacle of her eaten father and from her mother's bright-eyed lies, from all the maniacal respectability," from the "genteel, hygienic house in which she was forced to live a double life" (*CS*, 227–28). Kitty's escape is to sixteen-hour days of work, complaints, and inferior living conditions, but like so many young female protagonists, she has an asylum, a special place in nature that sustains her.

> Friendless, silent, long and exasperating, the summers, indeed, were no holiday. But she lived them in pride and without woe and with a physical

intelligence that she did not exercise in the winter; there in the mountains, she observed the world acutely and with love—at dusk, the saddle
horses grazing in the meadow were joined by deer seeking the salt lick;
by day the firmament was cloudless and blinding and across the blue of
it chicken hawks and eagles soared and banked in perpetual reconnais-
sance; by night the stars were near, and the mountains on the moon,
when it was full, seemed to have actual altitude. On these wonders,
Kitty mused, absorbed. (*CS*, 228)

A green-world escape and solitude help to deaden the dismal reality
of Kitty's life. Other protagonists, denied such solace, must confront
an unadulterated truth. In "And Lots of Solid Color," for example,
Marie Charles waits and prays for the letter that will bring her a
teaching job, but she is "trying in vain to make a new, clean daydream
out of the few desiccated hopes she had left." The unnamed narrator
of "A Reunion" is hoping futilely as well when she returns to her widowed, estranged father seven years after her youthful departure.
Widowed by his daughter's birth, the now elderly man has always resented his child but needed her too, for as she notes, "Who but I could
so often and yet so impotently threaten his exquisite obsession?
Whose guilt was so ineradicable?" The reunion is unsuccessful because the father is unforgiving; "his seven static years had done no
more than reinforce what had been there all along."[31]

Another twist on the theme of father-daughter relationships and
another young protagonist's disappointing revelation occur in "The
Bleeding Heart." Rose Fabrizio, a twenty-one-year-old Mexican girl,
has fled her miserable existence with her cruel, stupid father and has
lived in New England for two months. Lonely and envious of the cultured natives, she, like Sonie, wants to be adopted by a New Englander—specifically, by an elderly gentleman whom she sees regularly at the library. But her fantasies about the old man's gentility and
scholarly pursuits are shattered when she discovers that he is the
lecherous, seedy son of her bedridden, querulous neighbor, and when
he lasciviously asks her to the movies and suggests that she call him
"Daddy."

"A Reunion" and "The Bleeding Heart" share, along with the three
novels and many of the stories, one of the most pervasive themes in

31. Stafford, "And Lots of Solid Color," 22, and "A Reunion," *Partisan Review*, XI
(Fall, 1944), 425, 424.

Stafford's work. Although she occasionally examines the interaction between women (women as enemies, in "A Winter's Tale" and "A Slight Maneuver"; women as social creatures, in "Polite Conversation" and "Maggie Meriwether's Rich Experience"; women as allies, in "In the Zoo"), more often Stafford examines female characters interrelating with—and defining themselves according to their relationship with—men. A variation on this theme, developed through Stafford's examination of marriage, divorce, and spinsterhood, involves the other major male-female relationship in a woman's life— that between father and daughter.

Many of Jean Stafford's older women, particularly the unmarried ones, share an obsessive fascination with the memories of their male parent. Throughout "The Hope Chest," Rhoda Bellamy thinks of and even, in her mind, converses with her father, who has been dead for twenty years. It is her father who gave her a hope chest, because "nothing is too good for my Rhoda girl"; her father whose portrait hangs in the hall; and her father who is her only love: "Well, Papa, the laugh's on you," she muses some years before the time of the story. "Here I am, thirty-five years old, and in the eighteen years since I came out, I have had no beau but my dear papa" (*CS*, 113). Lucy Pride, in *Boston Adventure*, constantly quotes her revered father and preserves a library in her Boston home as a memorial to the long-deceased patriarch. In *The Catherine Wheel*, Katharine Congreve idolizes her scholarly father, whose character and looks she strives to emulate. Shortly before her death, she admits, in pain, that "only the Humanist loved me" (*CW*, 231). Whether these women's obsessions with their fathers is the cause or the result of their single state is not the issue; what Jean Stafford seems to imply is that women need to (or perhaps, to their disadvantage, tend to) identify themselves with and through a man.

Many of Stafford's younger protagonists' problems arise from the impossibility of having a healthy relationship with their fathers. Herman Marburg, in *Boston Adventure*, genuinely loves Sonie, but he is so unhappy with her mother and so demoralized by his inability to succeed at his craft that he abandons her. In his ineffectuality, he resembles Kitty's unemployed father, in "The Tea Time of Stout-hearted Ladies." Molly adores her father in *The Mountain Lion*, safely creating an image of a man who is dead. Fanny does not elaborate on her relationship with her father in "A Winter's Tale," but he does sacrifice her to the machinations of Persis Galt, and Fanny's introductory comment obviously characterizes the man: "My father, widowed by my birth, was an ascetic Boston Irishman, austerer and more abstinent than the descendants of Edwards or the Mathers. Wickedness engrossed him and its punishment consoled him; he looked on me, not without satisfaction, as his hair shirt, and my failure to receive a vocation pleased him at the same time that it exasperated him" (*BC*, 230). He could very well be the father in "A Reunion."

Stafford's women live in a man's world. Bright and sensitive, they recognize that their often unfulfilled, frustrating lives are inevitably defined and limited by men—who, neither bright nor sensitive, are often absent, ineffectual, or bullying. They exist in Stafford's stories because they exist in her characters' lives, but they are peripheral figures in her fictional world. She is far more concerned with their women and how they function in a world that belongs to men.

V
Orphans in Solitary Confinement
The Short Stories

As her novels and stories indicate, in technique as well as theme, Jean Stafford is interested in discovery, in the revelatory moment, in the burgeoning of awareness. Appropriately, of all her characters, her children most vividly and cogently present her world view. Handicapped by their youthful inefficacy and their limited knowledge and understanding, these young people are frequently put further at a disadvantage by less common circumstances: some are orphaned and unwanted; some (like Molly Fawcett) are precocious and misunderstood; and nearly all bear the double burden of being both young and female. As the titles of some of her stories about adult female protagonists indicate ("Children Are Bored on Sunday," "The Children's Game"), Stafford metaphorically associates women and children, who, as minority members of a male-dominated society, often share the bleak recognition that life is inequitable.

Yet, despite the intrinsic affinity between women and children in Stafford's world, ironically, her female protagonists rarely have children of their own. Angelica Early, Mary Heath, Cora Maybank, Mary Rand, Beatrice Trueblood, and May in "A Country Love Story" are all married and of childbearing age, but childless, and seem neither to consider having children nor to regret not having them. Perhaps it is because she herself (by necessity) had no children that Stafford did not attempt to recreate the experience of motherhood in her fiction. More likely, however, these characters' memories of the trials of childhood, as well as their adult perceptions of life, have made them reluctant to introduce children into this "improbable world." Certainly childhood memories are significant in many of Stafford's stories of adults.

The sudden snowfall in "The Philosophy Lesson" occasions Cora's memories of fetching Christmas greens with her brother and father, and sledding on a dangerous but thrilling hill (*CS*, 364–65). Her recollections in "An Influx of Poets" are less pleasant but more instructive: "Each Fourth of July night at Grann Savage's house in Missouri, before we moved to Colorado, my father had caught fireflies in one of Mama's hairnets and draped it over my older sister Abigail's head." As her younger sister watched, Abigail would dance and twirl. "I wanted a halo, too, but there was no other hairnet, and when I stamped my foot and shouted, 'It isn't *fair!*' Mama tried to soothe me, saying, 'Never mind. You can put it on when Abigail is through.'"[1] Polly Bay remembers the Fourth of July and Christmas too, as well as Thanksgiving and Sunday dinners at Great-grandmother's house, where "the Presbyterian grace was half as long as a sermon" and as dry as the fried rabbit, and "on reflection, she understood the claustrophobia that had sent her sisters and cousins all but screaming out of town; horrified, she felt that her own life had been like a dream of smothering" (*CS*, 309). Beatrice Trueblood's hideous childhood is so memorable, and the memory of it so powerful, that, years later, it accounts in part for her deafness; and Pansy Vanneman retreats to her childhood when she withdraws into the quiet, smooth envelope of her brain.

Technically, Stafford pursues the association between women and children throughout the short stories with imagery that highlights their shared estrangement. Those lonely, dependent women whom Abby Reynolds has joined in "The Children's Game" are described as pitiful children—"waifs" and "orphans" (*CS*, 22). Mrs. Ramsey, in "The Captain's Gift," is, in her ignorance of reality, "like a child, who,

1. Stafford, "An Influx of Poets," 46.

dressed in her mother's clothes, is accepted as a grown-up," and finally, like Molly, and like all other children, even this "innocent child
of seventy-five" must grow up (*CS*, 438, 440). Angelica Early is en-
couraged to preserve her innocence, and is as a result like a child; she
has a "girlish" and "innocent" mind, and her eyes have "retained the
pale, melting blue of infancy" (*CS*, 449, 450). At the end of her sad
career, Angelica welcomes her aunt by holding out her arms "like a
child, to be embraced," but rejects the woman's gift of gloves with "infantile fury" (*CS*, 461). And the aunt's pronouncement that "the child
had no memories" is for the most part accurate (*CS*, 462). In "A
Country Love Story," Daniel is ill and requires special care and consideration as he childishly withdraws from his wife and imagines her
guilty actions. Yet, ironically, he continually refers to May as a child.
He is described as a "professor catching out a student in a fallacy,"
and as "a tolerant father" who forgives the ignorant child who is unaware of its transgressions (*CS*, 139, 142). With many other writers,
one could simply comment upon the author's perception that women,
when they act irrationally, are like children. But Stafford's insight
into the complexities and problems of children forbids such a superficial interpretation. For Stafford, women and children, equally power-
less and underestimated, share a fundamental alienation from the patriarchal society in which they live.

Thematically, too, Stafford explores the special alliance of women
and children. Insentient and indolent, Mrs. Otis in "A Modest Proposal" has passed in the torpid Caribbean heat five of the six weeks
that will grant her a divorce. Unamused by her hedonistic host, Captain Sundstrom, whose idea of charm is to entertain his guests with
a yarn about "a perfectly cooked baby" that nearly provided the
"tastiest dish of his life," Mrs. Otis wanders to the garden with the
Captain's binoculars and peers at the beach; "almost at once, as if they
had been waiting for her, there appeared . . . a parade of five naked
Negro children leading a little horse exactly the color of themselves"
(*CS*, 73, 71). She watches the children as they frolic in the water, trying—with eventual success—to ride the horse. A sudden, violent
storm erupts, scattering the children and soaking Mrs. Otis, who
accepts a towel from the Captain's abused, cringing kitchen boy.
Vaguely she associates him with the children on the beach and the
roasted baby of the Captain's tall tale: "She observed that he wore a

miraculous medal under his open shirt. She looked into his eyes and thought, Angels and ministers of grace defend you. The gaze she met humbled her, for its sagacious patience showed that he knew his amulet protected him against an improbable world. His was all the sufferance and suffering of little children. In his ambiguous tribulation, he sympathized with her, and with great dignity he received the towel, heavy with rain, when she had dried herself" (*CS*, 74). The transcendent moment of recognition and sympathy that Mrs. Otis and the native boy experience is a rapprochement that only kindred souls could share.

One of Stafford's most successful stories, "In the Zoo," offers another perspective on the theme of women and children. Reprising the frame technique of "A Winter's Tale," Stafford in this story develops her thesis about the lingering influence of childhood events in the first-person account of the dolorous childhood of two sisters who, years later, as middle-aged women, have not obliterated the scars of their youth.

Like many of Stafford's children, Daisy and the unnamed narrator, her sister, are orphans, who at ages eight and ten are "sent like Dickensian grotesqueries—cowardly, weak-stomached, given to tears, backward in school," to a "possessive, unloving, scornful, complacent foster mother, Mrs. Placer," a boardinghouse operator whom Stafford ranks with Persis Galt on her "black list" of bad characters (*CS*, 285; *BC*, viii). As adults, the sisters live on opposite coasts, and as the story opens, the narrator is about to board her eastbound train in Denver after her biannual visit with Daisy, who has come from her home in the West to see her off. Awaiting the departure time in the Denver zoo, the pair recollect their childhoods in nearby Adams, an ugly, dreary town that spells unpleasant memories "with a legibility so insistent that you have only to say the name of the town aloud to us to rip the rinds from our nerves and leave us exposed in terror and humiliation" (*CS*, 285). It is, they realize, not Adams itself so much as its associations with the suspicious, malevolent Mrs. Placer that make the memory so horrific. Although remunerated by their father's life insurance for raising the girls, Mrs. Placer plays the selfless martyr, and *sacrifice*, the narrator remarks, "was a word we were never allowed to forget" (*CS*, 286).

The animals in the zoo trigger the flashback to the memory of a specific incident in the sisters' guilt-ridden past, when, to escape the cynical complaining of "Gran" and her boarders, the girls find solace in the company of Mr. Murphy, a quiet alcoholic who keeps a menagerie of a skunk, a parrot, and two monkeys. When Mr. Murphy gives them a puppy (which, amazingly, Gran allows them to keep), the sisters are thrilled. "He was our baby, our best friend, the smartest, prettiest, nicest dog in the entire world," rhapsodizes the narrator (*CS*, 291). But Laddy likes to roam, and when one day he returns from a "long hunting weekend in the mountains," Gran takes over, changing his name to Caesar and subjugating the dog as she has subjugated the girls, so that "before many weeks passed . . . he ceased to be anyone we had ever known" (*CS*, 292, 293). Mr. Murphy learns of Laddy's unwilling transformation into the vicious Caesar and confronts Gran, but before the man can vent his anger, Caesar attacks and kills one of his monkeys. Mr. Murphy has his revenge: the next day Caesar dies after eating poisoned meat. With Caesar dies the sisters' friendship with Mr. Murphy, and the girls remain in the insidious clutches of Gran. As they grow, the narrator writes, "Daisy and I lived in a mesh of lies and evasions, baffled and mean, like rats in a maze" (*CS*, 300).

"Why did we stay until we were grown?" wonders the narrator aloud. The Great Depression; no money; no place to go, suggests Daisy, "but it had been infinitely harder than that, for Gran, as we now see, held us trapped by our sense of guilt. We were vitiated, and we had no choice but to wait, flaccidly, for her to die" (*CS*, 301). The sisters escape eventually and never return to Adams, and the narrator assures us that the girls "did not unlearn those years as soon as we put her out of sight in the cemetery and sold her house for a song to the first boob who would buy it" (*CS*, 301). Now, years later, thrust into that dreaded past, and reliving painful emotions, the narrator states:

> We are heartbroken and infuriated and we cannot speak.
>
> Two hours later, beside my train, we clutch each other as if we were drowning. We ought to go out to the nearest policeman and say, "We are not responsible women. You will have to take care of us because we cannot take care of ourselves." But gradually the storm begins to lull.
>
> "You're sure you've got your ticket?" says Daisy. "You'll surely be able to get a roomette once you're on."
>
> "I don't know about that," I say. "If there are any V.I.P.s on board, I won't have a chance. 'Spinsters and Orphans Last' is the motto of this line." (*CS*, 302)

Affectionately, the women part, and on the train the narrator writes her customary parting letter to Daisy, which reaffirms that for them nothing can be as horrid—or, even now, as deleterious—as their childhoods with Gran.

As children, Daisy and her sister are typical Stafford characters. Orphans, like Lily in "Life Is No Abyss" and Jim Littlefield in "A Summer Day," they long for a conventional family life. Like Sonie and Emma, and like most of Stafford's other characters, young and old, the girls are misfits, out of place not only in Gran's petty world but in the larger world as well. Like Sonie, and Ralph and Molly, they are excluded from games at school; and they are conscious of their orphan status—a situation and a consciousness that are exacerbated by their sex: "'If only we were something besides kids! Besides girls!' mourned Daisy" (*CS*, 299). As adults they can avoid Adams and delight in Gran's absence, but the damage is irrevocable. When, on the train, she finishes her letter to Daisy and moves to the window to view the passing scene, the narrator betrays the inexorable influence of the cynical old woman. "They are alfalfa fields, but you can bet your bottom dollar that they are chockablock with marijuana," she muses (*CS*, 303). Her response to the recognition of her similarity to the dreaded Gran is silent laughter, "an unholy giggle," but the residue of Gran's contempt is not funny.

Another story of the exigencies of childhood, "Cops and Robbers," is deceptively complex, for it operates on several distinct levels. Like Henry James's *What Maisie Knew*, Stafford's story is a technical *tour de force* that presents a specifically adult situation (an unhappy marriage) from a child's point of view. It is as well a trenchant portrayal of a child's victimization by adults. Perhaps less apparently, "Cops and Robbers" compares the analogous situations of woman and child.

Five-year-old Hannah Talmadge, the youngest of five children, is the pampered pet of the family. Every morning she shares a grown-up colloquy with her mother, as the indolent woman leisurely brushes and curls her youngest daughter's long golden tresses. For a month Hannah has reveled in the attentions of a painter who labors each afternoon at a life-size portrait of the girl and her mother, with their identical silky curls. Hannah treasures her hair, for it alone guarantees her favored status as "the baby." In all else, she is an outsider in the family. Her siblings, ages ten through thirteen, were all too old and busy to pay much attention to her . . . and when family photographs were taken, they were sometimes lined up according to height; these were called "stairstep portraits," and while Hannah, of course, was included, she was so much smaller than Janie that she spoiled the design, and one time Uncle Harry, looking at a picture . . . had said, pointing to Hannah, "Is that the runt of the litter or is it a toy breed?" Andy, who was Uncle Harry's pet, said, "We just keep it around the house for its hair. It's made of spun gold, you know, and very invaluable." (CS, 428).

As the story begins, Hannah's *raison d'être* has been purloined and she, according to her mother, "has gone into a decline like a grown woman . . . sudden fits of tears for no apparent reason and then simply hours of brooding. She won't eat, she probably doesn't sleep" (CS, 423). Hannah's misery is occasioned by a dramatic haircut, her father's vengeance against her mother after a particularly virulent argument. Now the portrait sessions, which were for both mother and daughter a calm hiatus from the intolerable life at home, are ended, and Hannah's position as the family doll is threatened. Her siblings no longer pamper the girl, and "she felt that she was already shrinking and fading, that all her rights of being seen and listened to and caressed were ebbing away. Chilled and exposed as she was, she was becoming, nonetheless, invisible" (CS, 431). Her mother, preoccupied with her own bitterness, no longer lingers over her baby's curls, and Hannah wonders "how long they would keep her now that her sole reason for existence was gone" (CS, 428).

Hannah, the innocent victim of her parents' ironically childish battles, is typical of Jean Stafford's young protagonists, who in their inexperience, are vulnerable to the insensitivity of adults. Yet, although she is the youngest of Stafford's protagonists, Hannah shares many of the characteristics of her creator's adult female heroes. Hannah and her mother are both victims of a tyrannical husband and father, a blustering bully who does not "countenance contradiction from his children. 'I'm an old-fashioned man,' he announced every morning to his three sons and two daughters. 'I am the autocrat of this breakfast table.' And though he said it with a wink and a chuckle, it was clear that he meant business" (CS, 426). By the end of the story it is obvious that as Hannah's mother surmises, her daughter's predicament is a result of a displaced attack by her father on his wife. She moans to her sister, "How can one explain it away as an accident to a child when one perfectly knows that accident is not involved? Her misery makes me feel guilty. I am as shy of her as if I had been an accessory. I can't console her without spilling all the beans about Hugh. Besides, you can't say to a child, 'Darling, you are only a symbol. It was really *my* beautiful hair that was cut off, not yours'" (*CS*, 433). Hannah's mother is an accessory, but it is her father, Hugh, who bears the responsibility for Hannah's predicament. Her plight resembles not only her mother's but that of other women as well. Hannah could be Angelica Early at age five, treasured and applauded for her appearance, and learning that, without beauty, she is worth nothing to others.

Stafford captures the vicissitudes of childhood with wit and efficacy in a series of comic stories based on the experiences of Emily Vanderpool, a young resident of Adams, Colorado—a memorable character who, in her eccentricity and charm, is first cousin to Molly Fawcett. "A Reading Problem," which introduces Emily at age ten, begins, "One of the great hardships of my childhood—and there were many, as many, I suppose, as have ever plagued a living creature—was that I could never find a decent place to read" (*CS*, 323). Cast out of their bedroom by her sister Stella, "one of the most vacant people I have ever known," who practices ballet steps and campfire-girl songs; and banished from the library by a "fussbudgety" old librarian who "evicted children who popped their gum or cracked their knuckles, and I was a child who did both as a matter of course and constantly," Emily states that she cannot even find quiet anonymity in public places: "People . . . who are bored almost to extinction, think that everyone else is, too, and if they see someone reading a book, they say to themselves, 'I declare, here's somebody worse off than I am. The poor soul's really hard up to have to depend on a book, and it's my bounden Christian duty to help him pass the time,' and they start talking to you. If you want company on the streetcar or the interurban, open a book and you're all set" (*CS*, 323, 325, 324–25). Emily tries and rejects the train depot, the Catholic church, and the mountains before discovering "a peachy place—the visitors' waiting room outside the jail in the basement of the courthouse. There were seldom any visitors because there were seldom any prisoners" (*CS*, 326). So she spends her afternoons "more or less in jail," reading and memorizing the books of the Bible in hopes of winning a prize in Sunday School.

When one Saturday Emily arrives at the jail to find the sheriff, Mr. Starbird, burdened with some noisy prisoners, she is dislocated again. Wandering home, she rests by the creek in the tourist camp and is accosted by a strange, tall man in a black suit and a girl in a dirty nightgown who, spying her Bible, introduce themselves as traveling evangelists, father and daughter. The pair cross-examine Emily about her home and family in an obvious attempt to procure room and board for the night. And she, in her innocence, gives them the information. "It never occurred to me," she writes, "that I didn't have to answer questions put to me by adults . . . even strange ones who had dropped out of nowhere. Besides, I was always as cooperative as possible with clergymen, not knowing when my number might come up" (*CS*, 333). The strangers have just convinced her to lead them to her father's market for a sack of groceries when the sheriff—"like the Mounties to the rescue"—arrives and, exposing the team as frauds, sends them on their way (*CS*, 341). The sheriff credits Emily with the capture of the "hillbilly fakers" and drives the proud girl home. Emily's escapade "put an end to my use of the jail as a library because copycats began swarming to the courthouse and making so much racket in the waiting room that Mr. Starbird couldn't hear himself think" (*CS*, 343). Mr. Starbird apologizes to Emily for banishing her from her reading room, but, she writes:

> He wasn't half as sorry as I was. The snake season was still on in the mountains; Mrs. Looby [the librarian] hated me; Aunt Joey was visiting, and she and Mother were using the living room to cut out Butterick patterns in; Stella had just got on to pig Latin and never shut her mouth for a minute. All the same, I memorized the books of the Bible and I won the New Testament, and I'll tell you where I did my work—in the cemetery, under a shady tree, sitting beside the grave of an infant kinswoman of the sheriff, a late-nineteenth-century baby called Primrose Starbird.
> (*CS*, 344)

Emily is a year older in "The Scarlet Letter," but her life and her personality have grown no less troublesome. Virgil Meade is cursed with eyeglasses, and his valentine to Emily is insulting, but since "at that particular time I didn't have a friend to my name, having fought with everyone I knew, and the painful truth was that Virgil's valentine was positively the only one I got that year," she decides "that he was better than nobody" and accepts him as her beau. Their courtship, conducted over peanut butter, piccalilli, and mayonnaise sandwiches, reveals that "Virgil and I had a great deal in common; we both walked in our sleep and had often waked up just before we fell out of the window or down the stairs; both of us loved puzzles and card games and the two things in the world we really detested were Sunday school (Virgil said in so many words that he didn't believe in God) and geography homework."[2]

Emily is bedazzled by Virgil's tales of bravado, his hip slang, and his corny jokes; and when he proposes a petition against geography homework, "which was really ruining our lives and the lives of everybody else in the sixth grade," Emily, "ever his slave," seconds the idea. She agrees, too, to Virgil's suggestion that she sign her name as the author of the petition and present it to Miss Holderness, the geography teacher, since her recent award of a school letter for reading gives her a status that he lacks. The smitten Emily follows Virgil's advice to be unique and sew the red letter on her sock instead of the more traditional sleeve. This action strikes her family as disrespectful, and their protestations unleash one of Emily's famous tantrums.

> The devil at that moment made a conquest of my tongue and, blue in the face with fury, my eyes screwed shut, my fists clenched, I delivered a malediction in the roughest billingsgate imaginable, vilifying everyone at the table, all the teachers at Carlyle Hill, my uncles and aunts and cousins, my father's best friend, Judge Bay. The reaction was the same as it always was to one of my tantrums: appalled, fascinated, dead silence. When I was finished Jack [Emily's brother], awed, said: "Yippy-ki-yi! That was a humdinger of a one!" I threw my glass of water in his face and stamped out of the room. . . . Had anyone in the history of the world ever been so lamentably misunderstood?[3]

The petition is only a modest success, since a surprising handful of sixth-graders refuses to sign, but with a majority of seventeen names, Emily appears at school on Monday morning to find Virgil Meade noticeably absent, leaving her to bear the responsibility for the petition alone. Not only must she endure a lecture by the principal, two weeks of extra homework from Miss Holderness, and banishment to her room by her mother, but she must bear her classmates' interpretation of the scarlet letter on her sock as a betrayal of school spirit. Virgil, in the meantime, in the flush of the popularity he

2. Jean Stafford, "The Scarlet Letter," *Mademoiselle*, XLIV (July, 1959), 62–63, 64.
3. *Ibid.*, 66, 67–68.

has received in the backlash against Emily, eventually inadvertently admits that the "C" on the sock was his idea, and by the end of two weeks, Emily remarks, "I was in and Virgil was out. . . . Virgil, as it was fitting, was totally ostracized. In time I took pity on him; indeed, some months later, we again became boon companions, but I saw to it that he never hoodwinked me again: I ruled him with an iron glove and . . . ever after that Virgil Meade was the most tractable boon companion I had."[4] In "The Scarlet Letter" Emily learns that she need be no one's slave; the lesson, albeit presented more comically than those of Rose Fabrizio, Polly Bay, and Lily Carpenter, is no less cogent.

Like "A Reading Problem" and "The Scarlet Letter," the story "Bad Characters" begins with a forthright, arresting proclamation. Emily confesses the dreadful affliction, a Poe-esque "imp of the perverse," that controls her life.

> Up until I learned my lesson in a very bitter way, I never had more than one friend at a time, and my friendships, though ardent, were short. When they ended and I was sent packing in unforgetting indignation, it was always my fault; I would swear vilely in front of a girl I knew to be pious and prim (by the time I was eight, the most grandiloquent gangster could have added nothing to my vocabulary—I had an awful tongue), or I would call a Tenderfoot Scout a sissy or make fun of athletics to the daughter of the high-school coach. These outbursts came without plan; I would simply one day, in the middle of a game of Russian bank or a hike or a conversation, be possessed with a passion to be by myself, and my lips instantly and without warning would accommodate me. My friend was never more surprised than I was when this irrevocable slander, this terrible, talented invective, came boiling out of my mouth.
>
> Afterward, when I had got the solitude I had wanted, I was dismayed, for I did not like it. (*CS*, 263)

In "Bad Characters" Emily joins the ranks of rebels and misfits in Stafford's fiction. Her "difficult disposition" alienates her family as well as her friends, and she is more than a little proud of her prodigious temper. But Emily recognizes that she is out of her league when she catches Lottie Jump trying to steal a cake from the Vanderpools' kitchen. Nabbed in the act, the raggedy, ugly stranger pretends that she invaded Emily's house in search of a friend; Emily, who has recently irritated Virgil Meade ("I called him a son of a sea cook, said

4. *Ibid.*, 101.

it was common knowledge that his mother had bedbugs and that his father, a dentist and the deputy marshal, was a bootlegger on the side"), welcomes the companionship (*CS*, 266). Lottie, who does not know the traditional games, suggests the more intriguing pastime of rifling Emily's mother's bureau drawers. Only after secretly pocketing a perfume flask does Lottie propose a friendship pact and a Saturday shoplifting trip—three days hence—to the five-and-dime. Emily is mesmerized, as she had been with Virgil Meade, by the waif's "gaudy, cynical" palaver and seduced by "the daring invitation to misconduct myself in so perilous a way. My life, on reflection, looked deadly prim; all I'd ever done to vary the monotony of it was to swear" (*CS*, 269). Emily is, in short, smitten with her bold new friend.

The family uproar over the missing perfume flask and the chocolate cake (which Lottie liberates when, with the arrival of Emily's mother, she slips silently out the back door) unnerves Emily, and she is forced by circumstance into one of her ferocious tantrums to deflect attention from the thefts. But the diversion is temporary, and Emily, who "went to Sunday School and knew already about morality," is plagued with guilt over her impending crime (*CS*, 269).

> I had a bad character, I know that, but my badness never gave me half the enjoyment Jack and Stella thought it did. A good deal of the time I wanted to eat lye . . . . I didn't want to go downtown to steal anything from the ten-cent store; I didn't want to see Lottie Jump again—not really, for I knew in my bones that that girl was trouble with a capital T. And still, in our short meeting she had mesmerized me; I would think about her style of talking and the expert way she had made off with the perfume flask and the cake . . . and be bowled over, for the part of me that did not love God was a blackhearted villain. And apart from these considerations, I had some sort of idea that if I did not keep my appointment with Lottie Jump, she would somehow get revenge; she had seemed a girl of purpose. (*CS*, 274)

On Saturday, Emily and Lottie, who sports a tall, ridiculous hat, head downtown. And although Emily knows that Lottie looks absurd, and hopes that she will not see anyone she knows, "In another way," she confesses, "I *was* proud to be with her; in a smaller hemisphere, in one that included only her and me, I was swaggering—I felt like Somebody, marching along beside this lofty Somebody from Oklahoma who was going to hold up the dime store" (*CS*, 278). The two are natural partners in crime; while Emily distracts the salesclerk, Lottie lifts (and secretes under her hat) rubber bands, a tea strainer, rubber gloves, and "four packages of mixed seeds" (*CS*, 279). Then, as Lottie reaches for some beads, Emily's curious idiosyncrasy strikes, and suddenly feeling the need to be alone, she turns to and addresses Lottie and ruins the plan. Nonplussed, Lottie plays deaf and dumb, elicits the sympathy of the store manager and clerk, and leaves Emily—in a manner of speaking—holding the hat. Lottie disappears forever, while Emily endures the punishment of her father, the shame of her mother, and the teasing of her siblings. As the story ends, she reflects on her experience.

> It is not true that you don't learn by experience. At any rate, I did that time. I began immediately to have two or three friends at a time—to be sure, because of the stigma on me, they were by no means the elite of Carlyle Hill Grade—and never again when the terrible need to be alone arose did I let fly. I would say, instead, "I've got a headache. I'll have to go home and take an aspirin," or "Gosh all hemlocks, I forgot—I've got to go to the dentist."
>
> After the scandal died down, I got into the Camp Fire Girls. It was through pull, of course, since Stella had been a respected member for two years and my mother was a friend of the leader. But it turned out all right. (*CS*, 282)

Stafford contradicts Emily's proclamation that she has a "bad character." For her, the bad characters are the truly wicked—Persis Galt and Mrs. Placer—while Emily, she writes, "is someone I knew well as a child; indeed, I often occupied her skin and, looking back, I think that while she was notional and stubborn and a trial to her kin, her talent for iniquity was feeble—she wanted to be a road-agent but hadn't a chance. Her trouble stemmed from the low company she kept, but she did not seek these parties out; they found her. It is a widespread human experience" (*BC*, vii–viii). Emily and those like her are, in Stafford's words, "victims."

So, although the lighthearted tone and comic events of the Emily Vanderpool stories distinguish them from the bulk of Stafford's fiction, they are fundamentally similar to her more serious explorations of the world of the young. Limited in understanding by their youth and lack of experience, and trapped in their situations by the emotional, financial, and social impotence that they share with the dispossessed, Stafford's children are prey to the enmity and indifference of adults and the protean fates of her "improbable world." If Stafford is sometimes ambivalent about women, her sympathy for the young— and for the orphaned waif in all of us—is unadulterated.

VI
Style and Structure

Jean Stafford's ironic vision and modernist sensibility account, not only for her complex, ambiguous interpretation of the world, but for her concern for technique in fiction as well. Influenced by early-twentieth-century literary innovations that resulted from a new concern for stylistic craftsmanship, point of view, and objective narration, Stafford created work that critics and readers have long recognized as carefully constructed. Throughout her work Stafford attests to her interest in technique. In "The Psychological Novel," she reaches the conclusion that

> probably the reason writing is the most backbreaking of all professions is that it is so very difficult to tell the truth. Even though we may know certainly that our perceptions are accurate and that only one set of conclusions can be drawn from them, we are still faced with how to communicate the findings perceptively and conclusively. The language seems at times inadequate to convey exactly what we have seen and what we have deduced from it and much too often writers shirk their responsibility and take refuge in rhetoric—as the preaching novelists do—or in snobbish, esoteric reference, as Henry Miller and his followers do, in samples of language other than their own and in jargon, and in elaborate approximations that almost but do not quite say what they mean. But the language is quite able to take care of any of our needs if we are only affectionate and respectful toward it and, above all, patient with our-

selves: patient, not only in our hunt for the proper words themselves,
but patient in waiting for our observations to mature in us, to lose their
confused immediacy so that their timelessness will emerge and their
meaning will become available to our reader and applicable to him as
well as to ourselves.[1]

Her perception that meaning depends always on quality of language is evident throughout Stafford's work. And her particular fascination with language inspired nonfiction pieces such as "Plight of
the American Language," in which she denounces euphemisms; the
indiscriminate confusion of nouns and verbs; television, advertising,
and political cant—in short, the "linguistic buffoonery" of modern
American society. She calls for a "new kind of censorship" to be
effected by a board "made up only of persons demonstrably literate,
precise, immune to the viruses of jargon and whimsey, and severe in
their quarantine of carriers of the aforesaid." Stafford's fascination
with language (and the acquisition of her voluminous vocabulary) apparently began early in her life. "I . . . read the dictionary from the
time I could read," she stated. "My language was incredible." Language was to remain her avocation throughout her life. "To a certain
extent I *am* a philologist, undegreed as I am," she once wrote, "because language is and has always been my principal interest, my principal concern, my principal delight."[2]

Stafford's preoccupation with language is demonstrated in the
quality and diversity of her style—a style that, predictably, manifests
her complexity. Stafford, self-proclaimed progeny of two distinct
strains of American literature, employs with equal success the colloquial style of Mark Twain and the formal, rhetorical style of Henry
James. Stafford identified Henry James as one of her favorite writers,
and the influence of the master is obvious throughout her work.
Stories like "Polite Conversation" and "Maggie Meriwether's Rich
Experience" exhibit her interest in the social world of manners and
mores; others, like "The Echo and the Nemesis" and "The Warlock,"
share James's infatuation with psychological terrors; and innumerable

1. Stafford, "The Psychological Novel," 225–26.
2. Jean Stafford, "Plight of the American Language," *Saturday Review World*,
December 4, 1973, p. 15; Harvey Breit, *The Writer Observed* (Cleveland, 1956), 224;
Jean Stafford, "Miss McKeehan's Pocketbook," *Colorado Quarterly*, XXIV (Spring,
1976), 410.

other stories echo his curiosity about the unique dilemmas and insights of children.

Chester E. Eisinger calls writers of the "new fiction" (John O'Hara, J. P. Marquand, William Maxwell, Jean Stafford, and others)—with their interest in the inner lives of their characters, especially children, and with their dedication to craftsmanship—the "Children of Henry James," and proclaims that "Jean Stafford is the finest exemplar of the Jamesian tradition in her generation." For an example of Stafford's prose that demonstrates, in both content and form, the influence of James, one need look no further than the opening sentence of the first story in her *Collected Stories*. "Maggie Meriwether's Rich Experience" begins:

> There was a hole so neat that it looked tailored in the dead center of the large round beige velours mat that had been thrown on the grass in the shade of the venerable sycamore, and through it protruded a clump of mint, so chic in its air of casualness, so piquant in its fragrance in the heat of mid-July, that Mme Floquet, a brisk Greek in middle life, suggested, speaking in French with a commandingly eccentric accent, that her host, Karl von Bubnoff, M. le Baron, had contrived it all with shears and a trowel before his Sunday guests arrived at his manorial house, Magnamount, in Chantilly. (*CS*, 3)

The sentence is long and leisurely; the diction sophisticated, even archaic. Much of Stafford's prose is in this dense, textured, evocative style, which attempts to capture the detail and complexity of a modern, mutable world. In *Alternative Pleasures*, his study of "Postrealist Fiction and the Tradition," Philip Stevick contrasts the work of Jean Stafford, as a representative late modernist, with the fiction of postmodern writers. He analyzes Stafford's technique and sensibility as they are disclosed in the opening paragraph of "A Country Love Story," and reveals a style that illustrates "two principles, one a movement toward elegance when directness would seem to interfere in the wit and flair of the phrase, the other a movement toward embellishment in the interests of demonstrating an imagination expansively and leisurely at work upon its materials, comparing, supposing, qualifying, conjuring alternatives, musing."[3]

3. Eisinger, *Fiction of the Forties*, 294; Philip Stevick, *Alternative Pleasures: Postrealist Fiction and the Tradition* (Urbana, Ill., 1981), 35.

Stafford clearly shares "the introspective, contemplative, domestic imagination of the fiction of the fifties," and with her resonant style she can create a setting or character vividly, efficiently, and with rich detail and fresh images.[4] She captures the dreary aura of Abby's hotel room in "The Children's Game" with succinctness and perspicuity: "Abby's room, overlooking the sea and receiving the sea winds and therefore airborne sand, was papered with something nondescript, nubby and bilious, and the linoleum had been designed in the same mean-minded way. There was a varnished wardrobe, too short and shallow to hang clothes in, a wicker table with a crippled leg and a scuffed brown blotting pad and a rusty pen. The bed, with its tumid featherbed and its log of a bolster, was low, although its topography was mountainous" (*CS*, 28). Stafford manipulates her adjectival style and creates a crowded setting economically and vividly. In her hands, inanimate objects set up the mood and further the development of the plot with notable effect.

Her success with characterization is equally remarkable. Marianne Kimball's cabin-mate, in "The Warlock," is Mrs. McNamara, a fat, cheerful divorcee who seems "prepared for a long, domestic trip on a houseboat. She had a sewing basket and a loud alarm clock, a hot-water bottle, materials for giving herself a home permanent, for removing spots, for polishing shoes, for stretching gloves; she had a half-worked needle-point pillow cover, a pile of magazines, a knitting bag, a bottle of Scotch and one of brown sherry and one of blond Dubonnet. There were several boxes of chocolates and jars of sour balls standing about, and . . . salted nuts."[5] Throughout her work, Stafford's ability to capture the salient detail and her flair for the comic combine to create minor characters like Mrs. McNamara, whose appearances, albeit brief, are memorable. Stafford's affinity for the details of everyday life betrays the influence of the other major strain of American literary language. The colloquial style of Mark Twain and his literary descendants is utilized most often and most success-fully by Stafford in her novel and stories that are set—appropriately enough—in the American West.

"Woden's Day," extracted, along with "An Influx of Poets," from Stafford's unfinished novel, is her fictional portrait of her father—

4. Stevick, *Alternative Pleasures*, 35.
5. Stafford, "The Warlock," 26.

here Cora Savage's father, Dan. In the story Dan and the narrator share the comic, slangy style popularized in frontier literature and refined by Mark Twain, Sherwood Anderson, Ernest Hemingway, and others.

> Some years before . . . Dan had taken it into his quixotic head to go prospecting for gold in the Rockies. . . . He hadn't made his fortune, but he had had a larruping good time; that had been far and away a summer better than all summers before. . . . He had graduated from Amity College that spring, *summa cum laude*, and this holiday had been his reward. Mind you, if he had wanted to go to sea or go to New York City to explore the music halls and free-lunch saloons and Turkish baths, his father wouldn't have put up a red cent for a fandango such as that.

Years later Dan tells his children about the adventure and his companion, Thad McPherson, a college classmate known (because of his adeptness at Hebrew and the Jew's harp) as the Wandering Jew. His description of Thad illustrates Stafford's mastery of the colloquial style and her flair for dialogue: "Thad had a leaning toward The Almighty but Dan was an up-to-the-minute Darwinian and they had debated on this ticklish subject until the moon went pale. 'I'd try my level best to rile him, but old Thad was as mild as mother's milk. *His* theology had no more brimstone in it than a daisy. I think that old Wandering Jew was a B.C. pagan, believed in the wee people, believed in Santy Claus.'"[6]

As Tony Tanner notes in *The Reign of Wonder*, the vernacular style is particularly appropriate for first-person narration and the child's point of view. Stafford's accomplishments with the style in the first-person comic narration of the Emily Vanderpool stories affirm the validity of Tanner's thesis. "The Scarlet Letter" begins: "I knew from the beginning that Virgil Meade was crazy, but I didn't know he was a crook until it was too late and he had got me into a fine how-do-you-do that might have altered the whole course of my life. I mean I might have killed him and either gone to the gallows or spent the rest of my natural days in the pen."[7] The comedy and vitality of the Emily Vanderpool stories arise largely from the juxtaposition of styles, or more precisely, the intrusion of formal rhetoric

---

6. Jean Stafford, "Woden's Day," *Shenandoah*, XXX (Autumn, 1979), 7, 8.
7. Tony Tanner, *The Reign of Wonder: Naivety and Reality in American Literature* (1965; rpr., New York, 1967), 11; Stafford, "The Scarlet Letter," 62.

and diction into the colloquial. Emily is bright and precocious and, like Jean Stafford, has a remarkably abundant vocabulary. Her casual insertion of words like *insouciant* and *grandiloquent* adds an amusing touch to her stories.

Casualness, albeit studied, is the key to Stafford's style. She has, as Auchincloss maintains, "a poet's eye for the slang, the slogan, the comically vulgar detail that will suddenly superimpose twentieth-century commercial civilization on the dignity of the ancient past."[8] Her metaphorical language exemplifies Auchincloss' perception. Stafford's characters blithely echo contemporary cliches, adding a note of the mundane to Stafford's elaborate prose. Her father, Fanny writes in "A Winter's Tale," had "enjoined me to keep my nose to the grindstone until my declensions were letter perfect" and warns her that he will tolerate no "hole-in-corner monkey business" while they are parted (*BC*, 239, 232). Rose Fabrizio's father bathes "only once in a month of Sundays" (*CS*, 156). A car careens out of control "like a chicken with its head cut off"; even an attentive maid forgets her duties "once in a blue moon" (*CS*, 256, 245).

According to Eileen Simpson, Stafford shared her characters' fascination with everyday slang. "Her conversation," writes Simpson, "was studded with sassy expressions children used to use, and which she continued to use in her stories. Disbelieving what someone said, for example, she'd counter with a disdainful, 'In a pig's valise.' She weighed the phrase to make it sound as if she'd run through all the animals in the ark, and their valises—the giraffe's, the snake's, the parrot's—before settling on the pig's as the one that would best carry her meaning."[9] Her characters seem to choose their cliches carefully too.

Stafford occasionally adapts or combines cliches to create a vividly fresh, yet familiar, image. Maggie Meriwether is "miserable over the death grip in which the cat had got her tongue," a feeling that is exacerbated later, when, in the heat, her dress "began to look as if it had been dragged in by the same cat that had hold of her tongue" (*CS*, 5, 8). In "The Children's Game," Abby Reynolds' friend Hugh is "endlessly optimistic: around any corner at any moment, he might stub his toe on the pot of gold at the end of the rainbow" (*CS*, 24).

8. Auchincloss, *Pioneers and Caretakers*, 154.
9. Simpson, *Poets in Their Youth*, 121.

Stafford's manipulation of two stylistic traditions (and her clever reworking of cliches) underscores her ironic, ambiguous vision and her conservative interpolation of the past within her timely fiction. Similarly reflective of her complex attitude toward the past and present are her occasional deviations from her basically realistic technique. Jean Stafford worked within the "dominant fictional mode or consciousness of her time," Joyce Carol Oates writes in "The Interior Castle: The Art of Jean Stafford's Short Fiction." She further observes, "There are no experimental tales in the *Collected Stories* . . . no explorations beyond the Jamesian-Chekhovian-Joycean model in which most 'literary' writers wrote during those years. (Joycean, that is, in terms of *Dubliners* alone.)"[10] Critical opinion supports Oates's assertion that Stafford was a traditionalist, and the majority of her stories are traditionally realistic. It is, no doubt, Stafford's conservatism that accounts for her nearly undeviating adoption of "the Jamesian-Chekhovian-Joycean model." Yet, while not an experimentalist, Stafford the psychological writer does occasionally betray her awareness of, and appreciation of, late modernist innovations.

In Stafford's first story, "And Lots of Solid Color," published in 1939, Marie Charles awaits the arrival of a job offer. It is the weekend, and an aura of inertia hovers about the house, allowing Marie unlimited time for introspection:

> In the afternoon she sat at the dining room table playing solitaire. Passing the time, passing the time, for what, for what. Red jack on the black queen, maybe I will win it this time, if I win all kinds maybe it will mean that I will get a letter tonight. Not tonight. Nothing comes at night but Pacific coast mail. Air mail, yes, that comes too. Yesterday there was an airmail from Harry. *Father had a cocktail party at the club yesterday for my cousin who is leaving for London. I was very nostalgic for England . . . I hope your complacence continues . . .* As black is never white, so am I never complacent. What did he mean? Complacence? Ace of hearts and the deuce is in the deck. Seven of clubs, nine of diamonds, here it is, deuce of hearts. Yes, no, a letter, oh, please, please, I want the adobe house so much.

This extended, associative, interior monologue is more like those written by James Joyce in the more innovative *Ulysses* than in *Dubliners*. Another of Stafford's experimental tales is the *tour de force*

10. Joyce Carol Oates, "The Interior Castle: The Art of Jean Stafford's Short Fiction," *Shenandoah*, XXX (Autumn, 1979), 62.

"The Interior Castle." Six weeks after the automobile accident that has fractured her head and face, Pansy Vanneman, though healing physically, is rejecting rather than returning to a normal life. Pansy is obsessed with her brain, "which she envisaged, romantically, now as a jewel, now as a flower, now as a light in a glass, now as an envelope of rosy vellum containing other envelopes, one within the other, diminishing infinitely" (*CS,* 182). As her doctor attempts to repair her shattered nose, Pansy worries that he might maim her "treasure," might "leave a scratch on one of the brilliant facets of the jewel, bruise a petal of the flower, smudge the glass where the light burned, blot the envelopes, and that then she would die or go mad" (*CS,* 184). Of course, Pansy does not die, and does not go mad, but the price of the restoration of her nasal passages is her treasure. The poetic lyricism of "The Interior Castle," in which, to quote Hassan, "style is transfixed with meaning, captures the acute reality of consciousness."[11] The story is Stafford's most poignant statement of the terrible vulnerability of the intangible self to the ruthless assault of the exterior world.

Stafford's preoccupation with language, her concern for craftsmanship, at times results in an overdone, flawed style. Joyce Carol Oates admits, almost grudgingly, that "some of the stories . . . are marred by an arch, overwritten self-consciousness, too elaborate, too artificial, to have arisen naturally from the fable at hand (as in 'I Love Someone,' 'Children Are Bored on Sunday,' 'The Captain's Gift')." There are passages, in some of the stories, that seem precious, such as the following, from "Beatrice Trueblood's Story":

> Even when he was dancing, or proposing a toast, or fetching a wrap for a woman who had found the garden air too cool, he always felt on these occasions that he was static, looking at a colossal *tableau vivant* that would vanish at the wave of a magic golden wand. He was bewitched by the women, by all those *soignee* or demure or jubilant or saucy or dreaming creatures in their caressing, airy dresses and their jewels whose priceless hearts flashed in the light from superb chandeliers. They seemed, these dancing, laughing, incandescent goddesses, to move in the inaccessible spheres. (*CS,* 389)

Ihab Hassan agrees that "at its worst the style of Miss Stafford lacks resilience: it is brittle and brilliant, learned in chinoiseries and leger-

11. Stafford, "And Lots of Solid Color," 24; Ihab Hassan, "Jean Stafford: The Expense of Style and the Scope of Sensibility," 198.

demain. But then," he continues, "it is not very often at its worst." Elsewhere, in *Radical Innocence*, Hassan comments again on "the dandyism and refinements of style" in the fiction of Stafford and others, claiming that such excesses are "an attempt to preserve the integrity of language by removing it, perhaps too rashly, from the corruption of discursive speech in our age."[12] Stafford's conservative, proprietary attitudes about the English language, which she expressed in a number of nonfiction articles throughout her career, would seem to corroborate Hassan's assertion.

So rare are Stafford's stylistic lapses, so seldom does her prose deviate from its standard of clarity and realism, that the random overblown or inappropriate phrase is particularly noticeable. While most of her stylistic flaws are attributable to her sometimes excessive scrutiny of language, the occasional sentence that fails to ring true reveals at times an aberration of another of Stafford's technical preoccupations—point of view. For Stafford the modernist, psychological writer, and literary daughter of Henry James, point of view is a central feature of fiction.

In "The Psychological Novel," Stafford argues for flexibility of technique in fiction. "I do not think it matters what one writes about nor what method one selects to use," she remarks. "One may be altogether autobiographical or use none of one's own experience; it is equally good to innovate and to stick to the traditional rules; one may employ an omniscient observer or tell the tale without a guide. None of this matters if the eye and the ear, and therefore the pen, remain loyal to reality." Despite this disclaimer, however, Stafford throughout "The Psychological Novel" asserts her belief in the superiority of the distant, ironic author writing in the service of verisimilitude. "I do not argue, you understand, for happy endings but only for true endings based upon true premises, for that detachment from our characters' eccentricities and misadventures that prevents us from making them into improbable prodigies but that, on the contrary, enables us to be psychologically sound." All good novelists are psychologists, Stafford maintains, and "all good psychologists . . . remain impartial and do not sit in moral judgment upon their created people but allow the reader to draw his own conclusions."[13] Within the

12. Oates, "The Interior Castle," 63; Hassan, "Jean Stafford: The Expense of Style and the Scope of Sensibility," 200, and *Radical Innocence*, 103.
13. Stafford, "The Psychological Novel," 226, 220, 224–25.

parameters defined by Stafford's objective stance, her twin aims of revealing the inner life of her characters and disclosing the true nature of modern American society dictate her adaptation of point of view.

Like Mark Twain and Henry James, and Katherine Anne Porter and Carson McCullers, Stafford envisioned children as superior witnesses of the pathos, horror, and wonders of the world. Her presentation of the naïve point of view includes the first-person narration of the comic stories in her canon. Jessie, in "The Healthiest Girl in Town," narrates the story of her belated recognition that in a community of tuberculars and "ambulatory invalids," she, in her salubrity, is not the pariah that she feels herself to be. Her triumph is her proud announcement to her sickly, supercilious companions: "*I* am never sick. I have never been sick in my life" (*CS*, 216).

Stafford's employment of a first-person narrator in "The Mountain Day" heightens the effect of the epiphanic conclusion. Phrases like "in the self-conceit of my love" and "my obsessed and egocentric mind" bespeak considerable self-awareness, and throughout the story the reader—and Judy—are aware that this is a more objective, distanced narrator recreating a remarkably naïve eighteen-year-old. And yet, the idealism and enthusiasm of the ingenuous Judy are equally captured by the technique. Only with a first-person narrator could the objective Stafford write that "the berries I ate for breakfast came from the bushes of Eden" (*CS*, 235).

Stafford reserves the first-person narration for the comic, blithe experiences of her young protagonists, or, as in "A Winter's Tale," for stories in which the narrator-protagonist's revelation facilitates a valuable change in attitude. When childhood experiences spell fear and disillusionment, Stafford tells the story with a third-person narrator. Shy, homesick Duane's *Walpurgisnacht* in the dark protean streets of Heidelberg, in "The Cavalier," and recently orphaned Jim Littlefield's journey to a bleak, disease-ridden Indian orphanage in "A Summer Day" are related by an objective, third-person narrator. Similarly, Sue Ledbetter's relationship with schizophrenic Ramona Dunn; Ella's lonely, frightening experience with the eclipse; and Lily's introduction to her intransigent, acidulous Cousin Isobel are experiences so unrelievedly painful that the protagonists did not have the objectivity necessary to relate as well as experience them.

The anonymous, selectively omniscient narrator serves Stafford well too in those stories of the young in which she complements the education of the protagonist with a satirical presentation of the setting that inspires the characters' revelations. For the reader, "Maggie Meriwether's Rich Experience" is further enriched by the keen but objective eye of the uninvolved narrator. While the story is related through Maggie's eyes, Maggie, in her discomfiture, could not re-create her afternoon with the jaded European aristocrats with the perspicacity of the narrator. Similarly, the young scholars Malcolm and Victoria are too estranged and unnerved by their fellow teachers at the Alma Hetrick College for Women (where the goal of "preparing young women for the real job of the real woman, that is, home-making," is achieved in courses like "Marriage and the Family, Child Care, Home Ec, Ballet for grace, French for elegance") to portray them with the satiric eye of the narrator (*CS*, 76, 77). Malcolm and Victoria share the point of view in "Caveat Emptor," but the usually distant narrator intrudes to comment upon the deceptively sudden recognition of their love for each other: "Of course it could not have happened like this: falling in love is not an abrupt plunge; it is a grad-ual descent, seldom in a straight line, rather like the floating down-ward of a parachute. And the expression is imperfect because while one may fall one also levitates. Nevertheless, Malcolm and Victoria enjoyed the conceit of suddenness" (*CS*, 84).

Angelica Early is hardly more mature than Stafford's younger characters, and the narrator of "The End of a Career" is appropri-ately omniscient. An equally knowing narrator, objective and more perceptive than Mrs. Ramsey, relates the belated epiphany of the childlike grandmother in "The Captain's Gift." The epiphanic experi-ences of Emma in "Children Are Bored on Sunday," Dr. Pakheiser in "The Home Front," and Professor Bohrmann in "A Reasonable Fac-simile" warrant a straightforward, objective, third-person narration, but for the introspective self-examination of Cora Maybank in "An In-flux of Poets" and Jenny Peck in "I Love Someone," Stafford shifts to first person. While conforming always to her conviction that the au-thor must remain uninvolved in her characters' lives, Stafford adeptly manipulates point of view to best relate the story at hand.

Stafford's faith in the primacy of craft in fiction is evident as well in the shape of her stories. Her ease and facility in adapting a variety of points of view are paralleled in her approach to structure in her stories. As with her style, the structure of Stafford's fiction is so appropriate, so seamless, that the reader is rarely conscious of the hand of the craftsman. She juxtaposes a frame story like "In the Zoo" with the straightforward, chronological narration of "Polite Conversation"; she contrasts the slow, suspenseful delineation of character and plot in "The Echo and the Nemesis" with the breezy, satiric evolvement of "The Ordeal of Conrad Pardee."

Vision prescribes technique, and as an ironist, Stafford frequently juxtaposes pairs of objects—contrasting, examining, delineating the advantages and validity of each. In numerous stories, she contrasts disparate cultures, for example, the East and West in *The Mountain Lion* and in such stories as "The Liberation" and "A Slight Maneuver." Her year in Germany inspired echoes of Henry James's opposition of Europe and America, in "Maggie Meriwether's Rich Experience," "My Blithe, Sad Bird," "The Cavalier," and "The Home Front." The worlds of intellectuals and philistines are counterposed in "Children Are Bored on Sunday," "Caveat Emptor," "Polite Conversation," and "A Reasonable Facsimile."

Stafford's weary cynicism and modernist acceptance of the impermanence of human experience most clearly define the shape of her stories. More than half of Stafford's short fiction appeared initially in the *New Yorker*, the magazine whose influence on American short fiction of the twentieth century has long been controversial. Peden notes that "similarity of technique, subject matter, and tone have characterized a considerable amount of *New Yorker* fiction"; and while Stafford's work does exhibit some of the characteristics associated with those stories—the mannered style, the concern with twentieth-century urban culture—her perspicacious perceptions of modern American society lift her work above the superficial excesses of style that much of this fiction offers, sometimes exclusively. As Hassan writes, "In point of structure, [Stafford's] stories hold some affinities with a type we commonly associate with the *New Yorker*, though they hold more, when at their best, with the tradition of Joyce and Chekhov. The intimate glimpse unresolved, the moment of sudden knowledge, the reversal of a situation, the symbolic crisis, the humor of innocence and perversity, find each some deft application in Jean Stafford's stories."[14]

14. Peden, *American Short Story*, 22; Hassan, "Jean Stafford: The Expense of Style and the Scope of Sensibility," 199.

For the ironic writer the epiphany is the inevitable type of revelation; it is, as Northrop Frye notes in *Anatomy of Criticism*, "the theme of the pure but transient vision, the aesthetic or timeless moment." And Hassan corroborates that the modernist sensibility reasons that "our lives can take shape only in sudden epiphanies or isolated moments of crisis."[15] As a cursory glance at the conclusions of stories like "The Maiden" and "The Captain's Gift" adduces, Jean Stafford's short fiction, created in the tradition of Joyce and Anton Chekhov, is epiphanic.

15. Northrop Frye, *Anatomy of Criticism: Four Essays* (Princeton, N.J., 1957), 61; Hassan, *Radical Innocence*, 102.

Bibliography

Works by Jean Stafford

"And Lots of Solid Color." *American Prefaces*, V (1939), 22–25.

"Author's Note." *The Mountain Lion*. Albuquerque, 1972.

Bad Characters. New York, 1964.

"Bad Characters." *New Yorker*, December 4, 1954, pp. 42–51. Rpr. in *BC*, *CS*.

"Beatrice Trueblood's Story." *New Yorker*, February 26, 1955, pp. 24–32. Rpr. in *CS*.

"Between the Porch and the Altar." *Harper's Bazaar*, CXC (June, 1945), 654–57. Rpr. in *CABS*, *CS*.

"The Bleeding Heart." *Partisan Review*, XV (September, 1948), 974–96. Rpr. in *CABS*, *CS*.

Boston Adventure. New York, 1944.

"The Captain's Gift." (Originally entitled "The Present.") *Sewanee Review*, LIV (April, 1946), 206–15. Rpr. in *BC*, *CS*.

The Catherine Wheel. New York, 1952.

"The Cavalier." *New Yorker*, February 12, 1949, pp. 28–36.

"Caveat Emptor." (Originally entitled "The Matchmakers.") *Mademoiselle*, XLIII (May, 1956), 116, 166–73. Rpr. in *BC*, *CS*.

Children Are Bored on Sunday. New York, 1953.

"Children Are Bored on Sunday." *New Yorker*, February 21, 1948, pp. 23–26. Rpr. in *CABS*, *CS*.

"The Children's Game." (Originally entitled "The Reluctant Gambler.") *Saturday Evening Post*, October 4, 1958, pp. 35, 90–92, 94. Rpr. in *CS*.

The Collected Stories of Jean Stafford. New York, 1969.

"The Connoisseurs." *Harper's Bazaar*, LXXXVI (October, 1952), 198–246.

"Cops and Robbers." (Originally entitled "The Shorn Lamb.") *New Yorker*, January 24, 1953, pp. 28–34. Rpr. in *BC*, *CS*.

"A Country Love Story." *New Yorker*, May 6, 1950, pp. 26–31. Rpr. in *CABS, CS*.

"The Darkening Moon." *Harper's Bazaar*, LXXVIII (January, 1944), 60, 96–98, 100. Rpr. in *CS*.

"Don't Use Ms. with Miss Stafford, Unless You Mean ms." New York *Times*, September 21, 1973, p. 36.

"The Echo and the Nemesis." (Originally entitled "The Nemesis.") *New Yorker*, December 16, 1950, pp. 28–35. Rpr. in *CABS, CS*.

"The End of a Career." *New Yorker*, January 21, 1956, pp. 35–42. Rpr. in *BC, CS*.

"The Healthiest Girl in Town." *New Yorker*, April 7, 1951, pp. 32–40. Rpr. in *CS*.

"The Home Front." *Partisan Review*, XII (Spring, 1945), 149–69. Rpr. in *CABS*.

"The Hope Chest." *Harper's*, CXCIV (January, 1947), 62–65. Rpr. in *CS*.

"I Love Someone." *Colorado Quarterly*, I (Summer, 1952), 78–85. Rpr. in *CS*.

"An Influx of Poets." *New Yorker*, November 6, 1978, pp. 43–60.

"The Interior Castle." *Partisan Review*, XIII (November–December, 1946), 519–32. Rpr. in *CABS, CS*.

"In the Zoo." *New Yorker*, September 19, 1953, pp. 24–32. Rpr. in *BC, CS*.

"Intimations of Hope." *McCall's*, XCIX (December, 1971), 77, 118, 120.

"The Liberation." *New Yorker*, May 30, 1953, pp. 22–30. Rpr. in *BC, CS*.

"Life Is No Abyss." *Sewanee Review*, LX (July, 1952), 465–87. Rpr. in *CS*.

"The Lippia Lawn." (Signed "Phoebe Lowell.") *Kenyon Review*, VI (Spring, 1944), 237–45. Rpr. in *CS*.

"Maggie Meriwether's Rich Experience." *New Yorker*, June 25, 1955, pp. 24–30. Rpr. in *CS*.

"The Maiden." *New Yorker*, July 29, 1950, pp. 21–25. Rpr. in *CABS, CS*.

"Miss McKeehan's Pocketbook." *Colorado Quarterly*, XXIV (Spring, 1976), 407–11.

"A Modest Proposal." (Originally entitled "Pax Vobiscum.") July 23, 1949, pp. 21–24. Rpr. in *CABS, CS*.

"The Mountain Day." *New Yorker*, August 18, 1956, pp. 24–32. Rpr. in *CS*.

The Mountain Lion. New York, 1947; rpr. Albuquerque, 1972.

"My Blithe, Sad Bird." *New Yorker*, April 6, 1957, pp. 25–38.

"Old Flaming Youth." *Harper's Bazaar*, LXXXIV (December, 1950), pp. 94, 182–84, 188.

"The Ordeal of Conrad Pardee." *Ladies Home Journal*, LXXXI (July, 1964), 59, 78, 80–83.

"The Philosophy Lesson." *New Yorker*, November 16, 1968, pp. 59–63. Rpr. in *CS*.

"Plight of the American Language." *Saturday Review World*, December 4, 1973, pp. 14–18.

"Polite Conversation." *New Yorker*, August 20, 1949, pp. 24–28. Rpr. in *CS*.

"The Psychological Novel." *Kenyon Review*, X (Spring, 1948), 214–27.

"A Reading Problem." *New Yorker*, June 30, 1956, pp. 24–32. Rpr. in *BC, CS*.

"A Reasonable Facsimile." *New Yorker*, August 3, 1957, pp. 20–30. Rpr. in *BC*.

"A Reunion." *Partisan Review*, XI (Fall, 1944), 423–27.

"The Scarlet Letter." *Mademoiselle*, XLIV (July, 1959), 62–68, 100–101.

"A Slight Maneuver." *Mademoiselle*, XXIV (February, 1947), 177, 282–87, 289.

"Souvenirs of Survival: The Thirties Revisited." *Mademoiselle*, L (February, 1960), 90–91, 174–76.

"A Summer Day." *New Yorker*, September 11, 1948, pp. 29–35. Rpr. in *CABS, CS*.

"The Tea Time of Stouthearted Ladies." *Kenyon Review* (Winter, 1964), 116–28. Rpr. in *CS*.

"Truth in Fiction." *Library Journal*, October 1, 1966, pp. 4557–65.

"The Violet Rock." *New Yorker*, April 26, 1952, pp. 34–42.

"The Warlock." *New Yorker*, December 24, 1955, pp. 25–28, 30–45.

"A Winter's Tale." In *New Short Novels*, edited by Mary Louise Aswell. New York, 1954. Rpr. in *BC*.

"Woden's Day." *Shenandoah*, XXX (Autumn, 1979), 6–26.

"Women as Chattels, Men as Chumps." New York *Times*, May 9, 1970, p. 24.

"Wordman, Spare That Tree!" *Saturday Review World*, July 13, 1974, pp. 14–17.

Works on Jean Stafford

Auchincloss, Louis. *Pioneers and Caretakers: A Study of Nine American Women Novelists*. Minneapolis, 1961.

Avila, Wanda. *Jean Stafford: A Comprehensive Bibliography*. New York, 1983.

Baker, Nina Brown. "Jean Stafford." *Wilson Library Bulletin*, April 15, 1951, p. 578.

Breit, Harvey. "Jean Stafford." In *The Writer Observed*. Cleveland, 1956, pp. 223–25.

Burns, Stuart L. "Counterpoint in Jean Stafford's *The Mountain Lion*." *Critique*, IX (Spring, 1967), 20–32.

Chase, Richard L. *The American Novel and Its Tradition*. New York, 1957.

Chesler, Phyllis. *Women and Madness*. New York, 1972.

Daly, Mary. *Beyond God the Father: Toward a Philosophy of Women's Liberation*. Boston, 1973.

Eisinger, Chester E. *Fiction of the Forties*. Chicago, 1963.

Fetterley, Judith. *The Resisting Reader: A Feminist Approach to American Fiction*. Bloomington, Ind., 1978.

Flagg, Nancy. "People to Stay." *Shenandoah*, XXX (Autumn, 1979), 65–76.

Frye, Northrop. *Anatomy of Criticism: Four Essays*. Princeton, N.J. 1957.

Gelfant, Blanche H. "Revolutionary Turnings: *The Mountain Lion* Reread." *Massachusetts Review*, XX (Spring, 1979), 117–25.

Gilbert, Sandra M., and Susan Gubar. *The Madwoman in the Attic: The Woman Writer and the Nineteenth-Century Literary Imagination*. New Haven, 1979.

Goodman, Charlotte. "The Lost Brother, the Twin: Women Novelists and the Male-Female Double *Bildungsroman*." *Novel*, XVII (Fall, 1983), 28–43.

Hamilton, Ian. *Robert Lowell: A Biography.* New York, 1982.

Hassan, Ihab. "Jean Stafford: The Expense of Style and the Scope of Sensibility." *Western Review,* XIX (Spring, 1955), 185–203.

———. *Radical Innocence.* Princeton, N.J. 1961.

Janeway, Elizabeth. "Women's Literature." In *Harvard Guide to Contemporary Writing,* edited by Daniel Hoffman. Cambridge, Mass., 1979.

Kazin, Alfred. *On Native Grounds: An Interpretation of Modern American Prose Literature.* 1942; rpr. New York, 1970.

Mann, Jeanette M. "Toward New Archetypal Forms: *Boston Adventure.*" *Studies in the Novel,* VIII (Fall, 1976), 291–303.

———. "Toward New Archetypal Forms: Jean Stafford's *The Catherine Wheel.*" *Critique,* XVII (December, 1975), 77–91.

McClave, Heather. Introduction to *Women Writers of the Short Story.* Englewood Cliffs, N.J., 1980.

Review of *The Mountain Lion,* by Jean Stafford. *New Yorker,* March 8, 1947, pp. 97–98.

Morgan, Ellen. "Humanbecoming: Form and Focus in the Neo-Feminist Novel." In *Images of Women in Fiction: Feminist Perspectives,* edited by Susan Koppelman Cornillon. Bowling Green, 1972.

Muecke, D. C. *Irony.* London, 1970.

Oates, Joyce Carol. "The Interior Castle: The Art of Jean Stafford's Short Fiction." *Shenandoah,* XXX (Autumn, 1979), 61–64.

Peden, William. *The American Short Story.* Boston, 1964.

Pilkington, William T. Introduction to *The Mountain Lion,* by Jean Stafford. Albuquerque, 1972.

Pratt, Annis. *Archetypal Patterns in Women's Fiction.* Bloomington, Ind., 1981.

Rigney, Barbara Hill. *Madness and Sexual Politics in the Feminist Novel.* Madison, Wis., 1978.

Simpson, Eileen. *Poets in Their Youth: A Memoir.* New York, 1982.

Sokolov, Raymond. *Wayward Reporter: The Life of A. J. Liebling.* New York, 1980.

Stevick, Philip. *Alternative Pleasures: Postrealist Fiction and the Tradition.* Urbana, Ill., 1981.

Straus, Dorothea. "Jean Stafford." *Shenandoah,* XXX (Autumn, 1979), 85–91.

Tanner, Tony. *The Reign of Wonder: Naivety and Reality in American Literature*. 1965; rpr. New York, 1967.

Walsh, Mary Ellen Williams. *Jean Stafford*. Boston, 1985.

West, Ray B., Jr. *The Short Story in America, 1900–1950*. Chicago, 1952.

Index